THE MONEY PERSONALITY

$$$

THE MONEY PERSONALITY

A. E. van Vogt

$$$

Parker Publishing Company, Inc.
West Nyack, N. Y.

© 1972, *by*

PARKER PUBLISHING COMPANY, INC.

West Nyack, N.Y.

Library of Congress Cataloging in Publication Data

Van Vogt, Alfred Elton, (date)
    The money personality.

    Bibliography: p.
    1. Success. I. Title.
HF5386.V26   650'.1   72-6540
ISBN 0-13-600676-0

Printed in the United States of America

What This Book Will Do for You

After 40 centuries of hit-and-miss understanding of success, someone was finally lucky enough to notice what a financially successful human being—in terms of owning goods and property—has to be like. He has to have 12, and only 12, personality qualities.

The "naturals," who have owned and run the world until now, accidentally possessed (or possess) some or all of these 12 qualities.

Every one of the 12 personality qualities is described in detail in this book. Each one can be easily acquired.

Until now, your great problem has been *not knowing.* Your giant human brain needed a direction in which to go.

When you read Chapter One, and discover that one of the directions is "Become a non-victim," and discover also how you become that way, that's the moment you start changing. The remaining 11 qualities are equally practical—and equally basic.

In reading *The Money Personality,* you will quickly know and have:

- What it takes to charge a profit, and get it.
- The ability to focus your attention on money and not on foolishness.

- What to do to remain alert all day long.
- The information about where money is to be made.
- What you do to acquire a high financial and social IQ.
- How you can tell signals of success from failure.

And much, much more. As you grow each personality quality in turn, or sometimes all together, you'll be consulting the 12 chapters of this book, not only for the major qualities, but for these fine points, which, each time, will have more meaning for you:

- Why you should ask the price in advance.
- What your own personal reason for charging a profit should be.
- The three most important ways for staying awake all day long.
- How to discover from a game (of cards or sport) what your money reasoning is.
- How to tell if your husband or wife (prospective or existing) is a natural money personality.
- The first step in starting a business.
- The kind of warding-off thoughts to cultivate against failure or trouble.
- Where not to look for a mistress.
- How to take a nap, and exercise at the same time.

What was the nature of the "luck" that made it possible for me to obtain such precise information for the first time *ever,* anywhere?

Some years ago, I learned that three persons I had known well in my younger days had each in his own way become wealthy. At the time I began a study (as a cat might look at three kings) based on my intimate knowledge of their behavior as I had seen it in the child and the youth.

In this book I call these three men respectively **Mr. A, Mr. B.** and **Mr. C.,** A being oldest and C youngest.

From them I learned:

- Why some people suddenly lose their money.
- How to save 25% of what you earn.
- What kind of car you should have at what age and under what circumstances.
- The value of gifts.
- How to select a manager.
- What to do to regain interest in life.
- If you should or should not get even if someone does you harm.
- What emotion is sometimes a substitute for good health.
- The rules of money reasoning.
- The kind of mental energy it takes to create what never existed before.
- What fatigue may have done to your sensitivity and how to recover.
- What your philosophy should be.
- How to deal with your hidden security needs.
- Who to loan money to (when you have it).
- What to do about needy relatives and friends.

It's all here. In one short book. Virtually all the things you've ever wondered about in connection with making and keeping money (and about which you had no idea where to look for information).

Are you ready to come up out of that doped-off, non-money-making condition?

Let's go!

A. E. van Vogt

Table of Contents

A Victimizer's Delight . A Victimizer's Nemesis . Non-Victim Reactions . Making Yourself a Non-Victim . Male Victims Outnumber Female . The Money Personality Makes Clear-Cut Agreements, Usually in Writing, and Signed . Why People Are Victims . Peter Sellers Didn't Ask the Price in Advance . Avoid Getting Even . How New Are the 12 Qualities—a Comparison . Natural Money Personalities in Action . Methods of Salesmanship . Stopping Your Victimizers . Asking the Price in Advance

The Compulsive Assignment . Most Compulsive Assignments Are Not for Money . Receiving and Accepting Assignments Is Normal . The TV and Film Assignment System . Measure Your Ability to Accept an Assignment . Measure Your Ability to Give an Assignment . Moving Yourself Up the "Assignment Ladder" . Anger: the Emotion That Produces Both Low and High Assignments . The Best Assignments Go to Him Who Can Be Straightforward . Apathy

11

ing from Games . Learn to Add and Subtract Human
Nature . Observe Your Money Reasoning Ability in
a Game . Rules of Money Reasoning . Making
Qualitative Changes . What to Do at the Bottom .
Decide Which Type You Are . There Is a Method by
Which You, Too, Can Save . Your Response in a
Game Is Your Key to Business Reasoning . A Winner
at Games and Business

Competition Can Mean Many Things . Competing to
Win . Many Levels of Competition . Refusing Labels
That Limit You . First Unlabeling Therapy: Stop Labeling Yourself . Second Unlabeling Therapy: Refuse
to Label Others . The Difference Between a Label and
an Assignment

Nature of a High Social I.Q. . Key to Confidence .
Making Yourself Popular . Your Antagonisms Tell
You About You . The Really Great Men of History
Have Had a Common Touch . Basic Confidence Is the
Best "Line" . The Hello Scale

Some People Can Make Money but Cannot Keep
It . Finding Meaningful Interest in Your Work . Find
a Manager Who Has Quality Eight . Need for Meaning Not Relevant . How to Regain Interest in Life in
Two Steps . Hypnotism and the Twelve Qualities .

Other Realities . Meaning into "Moneymaking" . Occupations That Make Money . The Difference Between Rule Five and Rule Eight . The Essence of Quality Eight: Focusing Your Life . Personal Consequences of the Great Depression . Thoughts May Dim Your Desire

Using and Misusing Gifts . Choosing Each Day to Be Poor—or Rich . Turning Your Attention Toward Others . Gifts and Status . Ultimate Afterthought

Increasing Your Awareness of Signals . Signals to Heed in Businesses Big and Small . Learning How Fatigue Affects Signal Sensitivity . The Signals Known to Millions . The Three Stages of Fatigue . Surviving in a World of Many Signals . Signals Perceived by Scaredy-Cats . All Signals Are Received by Everyone . How to Respond to a Signal

Making a Habit of Being Decisive . Poor Decisions Often Have Hidden Reasons . Developing "Warding-Off" Thoughts . The Power of Stick-to-it-iveness . Making a Start . Begin with One Product . The Full-Time Job of Playing the Stock Market . Advice on Playing the Stock Market . Using Elegant Language . Staking Out a Stake . Habits of the Winner —and the Loser

12. **Twelfth Quality of the Money Personality: Escaping Orientation to Failure** **173**

Orientation Toward Dependency . What Your Philosophy May Reveal . Your Hidden Security Need . Stepping Out of the Orientation Glue . Using a Magical Crowbar Against Failure . Overcoming Problems of Victim Marriages . What to Do About a Non-Crowbar . An Alternative Solution . Dealing with a Severe Orientation Problem . How to Figure Out Your Orientation . Overcoming Problems of Victim Partnerships . False Victimizer Philosophies . Advice for Orientation Victims . Deciding to Escape a Mistaken Orientation . List of Possible Orientations . Your Orientation Therapy

13. **Your Own Money Personality** **195**
Your Twelve Qualities . How to Have Money and Be a Human Being

Bibliography of Success **199**

1

First Quality of the Money Personality: Assuming a "Non-Victim" Posture

In all commercial transactions, the money personality refuses to be a victim.

A few years ago there occurred an incident which was given wide publicity but which, so far as I was able to observe, nobody understood but me. And I understood it only in the context of the twelve personality keys to success that I am describing in this book.

The incident was the almost fatal heart attack that Peter Sellers, the British comedy actor, suffered while he was making a motion picture in Hollywood. Entirely apart from his touch-and-go bout with death, it is the aftermath that is significant in what I want to say.

He received a medical bill for $85,000.

A Victimizer's Delight

What happened to Peter Sellers had been happening to me on a lesser scale for years.

Example: Some years ago, I took a pair of trousers to a dry cleaners. When I arrived to pick them up, the tailor showed me where the cloth had been ruinously burned by a hot iron high up on the right side, and said, "You should have told me when you brought them in that you had burned them."

I was of course not guilty. But all I said was, "How much is it?" He told me. I thereupon paid him the full price for the drycleaning of my ruined trousers and left the shop intending never to return. And I never did.

But I was a victim.

A Victimizer's Nemesis

A few years later, Mr. C., the youngest of the three wealthy men whom I mentioned in my introduction, told me of taking his car to have a small portion of the fender repainted where it had been scuffed. When he returned to pick up the automobile he noticed at once that the workman had not matched the paints properly. However, the man presented his bill and apparently expected to be paid for his shoddy workmanship. Mr. C. went into instant anger. He yelled, "You take that damned car back into that damned garage and do that damned job over again—or no money!"

"Okay! Okay!" said the craftsman. And he did a perfect job next time.

Mr. C. was a non-victim.

Notice that there are two levels of victimizing in the foregoing. The burning of my trousers was an outright, brazen swindle. But the poor paint job on Mr. C.'s Cadillac was a far more common happening in our society. Outright victimizations occur in great quantities, yes; but every day, everywhere, both victims and non-victims in far larger numbers are confronted by low quality workmanship. Usually, whichever you are—victim or non-victim—you have to make up your mind on the spot whether or not to accept the poor work. Naturally, the victim accepts. The non-victim angrily demands that a better job be done or else he refuses to pay.

Non-Victim Reactions

At the moment of being a non-victim, the average person seems to be in a state of excitement that has the appearance of anger. His voice becomes high-pitched. He looks very much like someone who has stopped thinking and for the moment is simply reacting. What this suggests is that being a non-victim is in fact a neurotic mental process, which has never existed in the majority of people.

One of the persons to whom I described the twelve character points—of which this is the first—is a manufacturer whose business that year grossed $2,250,000. So he himself is an excellent example of what it takes to make money. He became very agitated when I described to him the victim/non-victim portion of my idea. His voice rose to a higher pitch. He protested excitedly that it was a grave error for anyone to show anger during a business transaction.

Since, as he demonstrated, it is so easy to misunderstand, I must differentiate. I agree that two business men discussing an important deal should not shout at each other—even though one turns out to be a sharp customer. But anger *is* the automatic reaction that I have observed in most natural non-victims. I might surmise that in such an untrained response we have a primitive defense mechanism. This suggests that a less angry reaction is possible. Therefore—

RULE FOR ACHIEVING QUALITY ONE

Cultivate a simple, straightforward, non-angry response by memorizing a few statements to make to someone who is trying to take advantage of you.

What should those statements be?

To begin with, let's discuss what they should not be.

At one of my lectures, a natural non-victim expressed himself as being disgustedly puzzled by my experience with the dry cleaner. He said, "Why didn't you just point out to the S.O.B.

that nobody brings in burned trousers to be drycleaned?"

A similarly baffled non-victim said at another meeting, "For Pete's sake, you should have let him know that it was up to him to be responsible for work done in his plant."

What is wrong with these remarks?

First of all, they show *total unawareness* of the victim's state of mind. At a moment of being swindled a victim is trapped by the victim's natural helplessness.

As time went by, and more such comments were made, it became obvious that victim, non-victim, and victimizer are entire mental worlds apart. They're all in a state, different but equally automatic.

For example, the comments I have quoted tell us what those two persons, as non-victims, would have shouted at the drycleaner in the high-pitched tone of voice which, as I have said, seems to be the defense mechanism of the natural non-victim.

A moment's thought will tell you that such responses are no help to a victim. They are attack-type defenses, and our victim is not an attacker.

They are accordingly not the kind of straightforward statements which a victim needs to make if he hopes to use Rule One.

What is a good example?

Making Yourself a Non-Victim

Mr. C. provided me with a high-level version. A man came to him with a plan for Mr. C. to invest Mr. C.'s money in a business which the man would operate. It quickly became apparent that the would-be borrower did not plan to offer Mr. C. any of the profits. Mr. C. was to take the risk of loaning his money, and if the business was successful he would get his money back. If the business was not successful. . . . The man avoided that aspect; he couldn't contemplate that possibility.

Mr. C. finally asked a single question, which I am sure should be standard in such situations. The question: "Since you are not a friend or relative—*what is there in this for me?*"

One man to whom I told this story protested its validity. "It's impossible," he said, "that anyone would try to borrow money on such a basis without realizing that he would have to give Mr. C. a large share of the profits."

This man is wrong. People *are* that subjective.

We may analyze from his comment that he is not himself a victim—and accordingly cannot grasp the variety of irrational human behavior in relation to money.

Unquestionably, there are thousands of people who want to borrow money to go into business, and who are quite willing to share the profits. I'll tell you in my discussion of Quality Five which of these people to loan money to, if you are an investor.

What I have been trying to establish is that the natural victim, the natural non-victim, and the (natural?) victimizer are all equally caught up in their own thing, are all equally emotional. But in each case it's a different emotion.

So any straightforward statement in dealing with a victimizer must do two things.

First, it must be simple, so that the victim-type can actually speak it in spite of the state of mind *he* is in.

And, second, it must have the power to penetrate through the heavy emotion of the victimizer and contact the thinking part of his brain.

We observe that Mr. C. in his situation asked a question: "But what is there in this for me?" It was exactly the right, straightforward question to snap the would-be victimizing borrower out of his self-absorption.

With these various thoughts as background, here now are straightforward type statements for my swindling dry cleaner and similar small-scale (non-crook) victimizers:

BASIC NON-VICTIM QUESTIONS

"What do you suggest we do?"
"How do you think we should handle this?"
"What is your solution for the problem?"

Notice that these are all questions, and none contains an accusation.

A question has the least attack aspect, and it is the best method of reaching a listener's brain.

Please note: According to Rule One *you must memorize* the foregoing questions, or variations that fit your character, in advance.

My suggestion: Write them on a card. Carry the card with you until you are no longer a victim.

Once you, as a victim, have broken your inner barriers by asking a question, you may quickly find yourself in a normal conversation that you can handle.

If not, if the victimizer intransigently continues his attack-attitude and you are overwhelmed, you may discover that you feel a lot better simply because you did ask the question.

My experience: Each time you ask it, it's easier.

Male Victims Out-Number Female

I estimate that 80% of men are victims on a confrontation basis and that 80% of women are non-victims. That is, most women can challenge poor workmanship or resist victimization and demand that justice be done. The average male cannot do this.

It would seem as if the wrong person is out there in the marketplace trying to make money.

A male friend to whom I gave these figures disagreed instantly. He said, "Have you ever seen a pack of women charge into a store to buy a discounted item? Women are the perennial soft touches for that kind of swindling; in other words, they are victims." My reply was that he had done all too quickly what has kept money-making unscientific: he had connected two different qualities.

Women are often soft touches when it comes to clothes, so-called bargains, and wanting to believe the sweet words that men say to them. But this is not in the same category as confronting a victimizer and demanding that he live up to his agreement. It's what you do when you have to look the other person in the eye that tells the real story.

The Money Personality Makes Clear-Cut Agreements, Usually in Writing, and Signed

Having been a victim myself, I can say without qualification that most victims are sad cases when they're being taken. I have had the experience of questioning persons who, at the time I talked to them, were in the process of being swindled. One example: Under my close questioning, the man described his deal to me. He gave a glowing account of the transaction. He was building a machine for a manufacturer. When it was finished, they would share the profits from its production. I said, "All right, have you got that in writing?" His answer, "Oh, yes."

It turned out that he had written it himself in the presence of the other person; he had taken notes, so to speak. Then he had read these notes out loud to the other party, and asked him if that was indeed the agreement. The man said, yes, it was.

The work would be done in the partner's factory, and our victim would receive weekly advances while he was constructing the machine—just like a salary, it seemed to me. But he protested that it was clearly understood that that was not so.

It turned out that my friend had not had the nerve to ask the victimizer to initial the agreement.

The day came when all the bugs had been ironed out of the finished machine, and it was starting its enormous output at the rate of $1600 a day. On this day the other man came to my friend's desk and told him he was fired. He admitted later that he had had an uneasy feeling all the while that he was not properly protected and that what he was doing might be regarded as salaried work.

My direct and detailed questioning, however, had not persuaded him to reveal these secret fears or to bring out the facts of the matter. That gives us a saddening picture of how powerful is the emotional force that works inside the victim-type.

Although we do not need to know why a victim is what he is, it is interesting to speculate on possible underlying causes.

Why People Are Victims

I used to think I was a victim because I couldn't bring myself to hurt the feelings of other people. Next, I decided that possibly the reason was my self-esteem. We victims, I analyzed, are really secret kings and queens. We cannot demean ourselves by any kind of self-defense in the presence of a rude fellow or swindler. My next thought was that this kingship is a form of compensating fantasy to conceal the fact that a victim, being really nothing, has no inner right to defend himself. Indeed, as I have illustrated, he often connives to be a victim. Perhaps, to use a psychoanalytic concept, he is expiating some guilt. Or it could even be that he is the sibling who lost the struggle to win mother from brother or sister, and he keeps dramatizing his loss.

Many people pretend to be victims, so being a victim must be a psychologically safe position. This was graphically brought home to me a few years ago when I accidentally ran into a retired grocer from a neighborhood where I used to live. He admitted he was in good health. But when I politely asked how things were otherwise, he started to pull a long face and act like a poor person. I was amazed and stopped him. I said, "Just a minute, sir. I heard that during your thirty years in that grocery store you bought up all the property in the block. Isn't that true?"

He became very pale and answered in a high-pitched voice, "But everybody likes me. Everybody likes me."

It would seem that need for approval may play a bigger role in our behavior than we victims like to believe.

If you want to make money, such a need has to be modified in the direction of straightforwardness, as I have already described it.

A victim says, "I want to get to the place financially where I don't have to ask the price." You'll never hear a non-victim make a statement like that.

Peter Sellers Didn't Ask the Price in Advance

Which brings us again to Peter Sellers, whose experience with the medical profession I described at the beginning of this section.

Some while before Sellers was so neatly taken, I made the following prediction to my money-talk audiences: "One of these days someone like Nelson Rockefeller will suddenly fall ill away from home, say in Chicago, and will be rushed to a hospital, with the most famous M.D.'s called in on the case. The illness will be of such an emergency nature that nobody will ask any questions in advance. When it's all over, he will be presented with a bill for *one million dollars.*

"And he won't be able to say a word. Because in our society, a medical group can charge according to ability to pay."

After my lecture on that occasion, somebody came up to me and said, "Do you know what would actually happen if Nelson Rockefeller became seriously ill in Chicago?" I said, "What?" He said, "That same day somebody from his office in New York will fly to Chicago, talk to the hospital authorities, talk to the doctors that have been called, make the arrangements, discuss every detail in the presence of witnesses and create a total non-victim situation for Mr. Rockefeller."

My answer was that that would certainly be the ideal development for anyone in the position that I had described, but that in my opinion one of these days some well-to-do person was going to be really unwary.

That's what happened to Peter Sellers, who was unwary and who as a result got knocked down for $85,000 when he had his heart attack.

Sellers, you may recall, wrote back: "My heart stopped eight times when I saw your bill," which I thought was a pretty good remark. But nonetheless he paid the $85,000.

Avoid Getting Even

There is a tendency on the part of non-victims to get even. As the non-victim thinks over what the other person tried to do to him, he becomes progressively filled with righteous anger and the determination to strike a balance.

Since the majority of non-victims are women, I wouldn't be surprised if this compulsion to get even were the cause of the kind of lifelong feud that two women can get into. Such a feud is extremely painful to their friends, since everyone has to be careful not to invite them to the same function.

My feeling is that getting even brings into a play a pattern that is not necessary to the victim/non-victim cycle. In my view, being a non-victim completes the cycle.

I think the factor that is confused here is something that comes under the heading of "teaching the other person a lesson." In effect, you say to him, "You have done something improper to me." (This could include swindling.) "Now, I'm going to show you that actions like that do not pay. You're going to learn that there are consequences to the kind of thing you tried to do to me."

My observation: Most of the time and effort spent on the teaching of lessons to other adults is wasted. And, besides, you may run into the same type of non-victim as yourself, whereupon he proceeds to get even with you.

Getting even probably has its place in the heirarchy of life's actions, but it doesn't belong in the realm of moneymaking—so far as I can determine. I read recently that in Boston, where John F. Kennedy grew up, the politician's credo was: "Don't get mad; get even." My suggestion: "Don't confuse what one has to do to keep people in line politically with what one has to do to make money."

How does one cease to be a victim?

It's not easy.

But I suggest that, having read this far, you will never again be quite the same kind of victim you were in the past.

In addition to this automatic change, I recommend what has gradually worked for me. Start by cancelling out having been a victim whenever it has happened. Take the item back. Or, if you have accepted poor workmanship, return and ask to have a better job done. Do this even if you don't mind very much. You're trying to break a habit, so don't give yourself an argument in favor of being victimized.

As soon as you can nerve yourself, ask the details in advance. You'll discover, alas, that that's a whole swindling world in itself. Getting the real, final price out of some victimizers is like pulling teeth. But after a while it gets to be kind of interesting.

Please note again that what I'm describing is not *how* to make money, but what sort of person you have to be before you can make it or keep it.

Becoming a non-victim is high on the list.

How New Are the Twelve Qualities?—A Comparison

Isn't what I've just told you different from anything you've ever heard in connection with moneymaking?

Not another scheme, not a lying method for a shady sale of doubtful value. Simply and forthrightly, *you learn to become a non-victim.*

The change is in you, and to the exact degree that you do change you handle that part of your life better.

Can I prove that what I have said is intensely relevant? And brand new?

In a way it doesn't have to be proved. I'll wager you'll be grappling with that idea from now on, veering progressively more in the direction of not being a victim; learning to be that way graciously and confidently.

Three years after I began my money study, at a time when I still had not arrived at a single conclusion, I was visited by a Master Salesman. He had read a book which I had some years before ghosted for a psychologist—a book on hypnotism.*

He wanted me to write for a corporation of which he was vice-president, a course of twelve lessons on how to be a success and a moneymaker. He would furnish the material; I would write it.

The course which I was to write, on the basis of material furnished me by the Master Salesman, was to be a psychological adjunct to a nutritional program which they planned to sell nationwide through franchised dealers. Unfortunately, when they were already starting to let contracts to vitamin firms, the Food and Drug Administration began one of their occasional, largely untruthful harassments of all hard-sell nutritional supplement

---

* *The Hypnotism Handbook,* by Charles E. Cooke and A. E. van Vogt, Borden Publishing Company, Alhambra, California.

deals—and my contact's superior, a 20-corporation president, got cold feet and backed out of the project. With the money backing gone, the whole scheme collapsed.

I am summarizing this experience because it pulled me out of my armchair, and for five months I watched men of action prepare a moneymaking enterprise.

Natural Money Personalities in Action

Translated into the language of the twelve qualities, I had the opportunity to watch people who had those qualities, do, think, and be, while it was happening. At the time, since, as I have already mentioned, I still had none of the ideas that are described in this book, I merely observed passively. Later, looking back, I realized they were high-level naturals.

The president of those numerous corporations, several of which had to do with land development, was once quoted by the Master Salesman as having said to another wheeler-dealer: "Now, Martin, what would be your opinion of me as a businessman if I accepted the price you have just asked me to pay?"

The subject being discussed was a large area of land in New Mexico which the would-be buyer planned to divide into small acreages and sell to investors.

You can see that his was a non-victim question of the type that I have been describing. And it immediately made possible the suggesting of offers and counteroffers on a realistic basis.

In one sentence he reached past the madness of the first quoted price.

After it was all over, looking back on my experience with these high-level men I realized that neither the 20-corporation president nor the Master Salesman ever noticed the practical methods they used. The course that I wrote for them was a stereotype of its kind, built around hypnotic records. The written material consisted principally of printed pep talks.

Methods of Salesmanship

The Master Salesman was a remarkable, knowledgeable man. His study of the literature of psychology had led him to a series of concepts about selling which caused a leading building contractor to describe him in my presence as the "most outstanding and successful sales lecturer west of the Mississippi."

These are powerful words. They came from a former professor of economics who had become executive vice-president of a company that was building an entire city.

One of the achievements of the Master Salesman was that he had figured out how to tie Freud's complex ideas into selling campaigns. Yes, there he stood before a seated group of men and women—most of whom had never even heard of the great psychoanalyst—and down into their nonintellectual minds he projected a fascinating version of Freud's ego, id, and super-ego concepts.

And what's more they held still for it. I'm not prepared to evaluate how good it would be for business people to rid themselves of personal problems a la Freud. Unfortunately, a typical Freudian analysis lasts from three to ten years and costs a fortune.

So, obviously, an education and psychotherapy are not what he was giving them. My impression then was that it was a pep talk. Later, after I began to understand these phenomena, I asked myself: But what is a pep talk?

The so-called pep talk, as you may know, has been an adjunct of salesmanship from early days. The boys come in at 8 A.M. They get a dynamic pitch from the sales manager, and away they go. In some fields this is done every day.

My analysis on the basis of the twelve qualities: These salesmen already had a number of the qualities, and a "pep" talk was actually an unknowing method of injecting Quality Eight. It was a method of making what they were doing real again to people who were tired, who had been rejected a number of times, and who needed acceptable supportive ideas to overcome the apathy which descends on the best of us when we fail.

The Freudian hoopla was indeed outside of their experience and true understanding. But it sounded as though they were being given a direct, close-up look inside the prospective land buyer's skull.

And so they lifted their heads again, breathed in oxygen and certainty, and the feeling that somebody—the management—cared because they had brought in for a fee the Master Salesman to tell them how it all was, really. Charged up once more they thereupon sallied forth into that arena of life where salesmen do battle with the rest of us.

But you can see that a basic solution for you has to be easier than that. And it is.

You're reading it. Your first step is to become a non-victim.

One note of caution: If you are a natural non-victim, don't intensify the trait. Naturals have a strong tendency, given the go-ahead signal, of becoming so obnoxiously non-victim that the distinction between what they do and what a victimizer does ceases to be clearly visible.

Stopping Your Victimizers

The money personality obtains real value for his services.

A young draftsman drew the plans for a house for so-called friends who talked vaguely of how this could lead to big things. When he finished the plans—which took him three weeks of full-time work—they merrily presented him with a bottle of champagne. When the young draftsman arrived home and told his wife what had happened, she smashed the bottle and its contents into the sink.

The young man was a victim. His wife, being a non-victim, promptly phoned the victimizing couple, demanded money, and got a check for $200.

During the course of my money study, I ran into an almost unending number of little stories like this, of small victimizations. One young couple, newly married, met an older man on the day of their arrival in the lobby of the hotel where they were honeymooning. A fairly harmless, congenial type, he came up to their room with them, and, as the evening lengthened, curled himself up on the sofa, said, "Don't mind me, kids!" and was soon snoring.

Three days later, when the mother of the groom phoned them long distance, something about their tone of voice signaled something wrong to her; she promptly took a plane and soon had the leech out on his ear. But in that three days this fellow, by borrowing, or by eating meals which they paid for, had used up half their honeymoon money.

Now, I could probably analyze for you in great detail what is the state of mind and the subjective philosophy of various types of victimizers. Some of the cases I ran into are very touching and have their own human-interest aspects.

But victimizers are not curable as a group, and there are millions of them.

So it's up to you to become a non-victim. How? As I've already said, it's not easy—as the following sum-up story demonstrates:

Asking the Price in Advance

A friend who had heard one of my talks on the money personality wanted a cover and a liner for the container of a phonograph record. For this purpose he went to the office of a company which did that kind of specialized printing, explained his requirements, and was quoted a price of $150 for 1,000 sheets for each side, a total of 2,000 sheets.

Remembering my advice, he took his non-victim precautions, which by then were almost automatic. The dialogue was as follows:

Friend: "That's the full price?"
Printer: "Yes."
Friend: "You have quoted me a price of $150 for this job, and that's it?"
Printer: "Correct."
Friend: "When I come back here three days from now, I'll write you a check for $150 plus sales tax, and that will be the full cost?"
Printer: "Yes, exactly."

Something about the printer's manner as he made these positive affirmations bothered my friend, so he said, "Let me think it over and I'll call you."

He went out, phoned an advertising agent who had already done some work for him, and told him the circumstances. The agent called the printer and discovered that the cost which had been quoted was for setting the type only. The charge for running off—i.e., printing—the 2,000 sheets (1M of liners and 1M of covers) would be an additional $150. The total cost in other words would be $300.

The ad-man added, "I'm sure I can get you the whole job done in the valley for about $150," which he subsequently did.

My friend later asked him, out of curiosity, "What question did you ask this printer that got you such accurate information?"

His reply: "I asked what exactly you would get for the $150 he had quoted you."

An obvious question, yet green, or learning, non-victims tend not to think of everything. I feel now that my friend's questioning, as far as it went, had the printer on the verge of leveling with him and that if he had asked him the same non-victim question the man would have come through with the facts for him, also.

One final thought: It may seem to you that some modern swindlings are just not worth the time and effort to circumvent. This is a wrong attitude, because—"Big trees from little acorns grow."

The beginning non-victim may save only a few dollars at first. But there is an attitude about a non-victim which prevents, or discourages, victimizing on all levels. Think and be a "non-victim" and you will stand straighter psychologically.

This one step is part of the overall pattern you need to achieve.

Develop a total non-victim posture is the first step.

Now, let's take the next.

2

Second Quality of the Money Personality: Giving "Money" Assignments

The money personality sets himself assignments he intends to carry out, with a moneymaking potentiality in them.

It is a truth that some people will do a specific task to which they are assigned—if they get paid for it.

Yes, millions of individuals actually carry out assignments that often involve hard labor over long hours without having a personal interest in the task itself. They do it for the money alone.

For the vast majority of people, the amount of money involved in the assignment he (she) has accepted provides a minimum living.

This is not the assignment level at which the money personality constantly seeks to operate.

Is your reaction to the foregoing, "Of course; so what's new?"

Well, that's one of the aspects of the twelve qualities: they're not new. In fact, when you finally learn what they all are, you'll see them sticking out or poking at you from all over the place.

But what you are reading *is* the first time ever that somebody is saying to you: *"That* obvious thing over there. Take a good look at it. *It* is important." Meaning, some other equally obvious things are not important—to money.

Undoubtedly there are realities in life besides money. Art, literature and culture. Desirable women and attractive men. Beauty and nature. Stimulating games, healthful activities, and joyous moments.

This book is not about these things. This book is about money.

And Quality Two has to do with strengthening your ability to seek assignments that lead you to money.

I want to make that crystal clear.

There are two kinds of assignment, essentially. The one I've just described—whereby an employer gives somebody a task to do, and pays him for it—is the most common and usually the least profitable to the assignee (you).

The second type of assignment is the one you either give to yourself consciously, or are driven to by an unknown force within you.

The Compulsive Assignment

It is very likely that some artists and writers receive an assignment from within.

John Brunner, English writer (principally of psychological science fiction), is probably the most productive new writer in the world today. In 18 years of professional authoring, he has written nearly 60 novels and hundreds of short stories and novelettes. All of this high-speed production is good; a lot of it is excellent; some of it (*Stand on Zanzibar, The Whole Man, The Jagged Orbit*, to name a few) is outstanding.

I met Brunner a couple of years ago and asked him if what I had heard was true—that he could on occasion write one of his unusual novels in ten days. His answer: "Yes, but. . . ."

The "but" was that he did not write a novel every ten days. He had his advance thinking periods when, apparently, he did nothing but enjoy life: visit friends, travel, read. But the new novel (or short story) was gestating during those periods. Suddenly—and that was the impression I got of what happened—an inner excitement would begin. A feeling, strong, irresistible; an absolute pressure, urging him to start to set words down on paper.

Somewhere in this stage (if it was a novel) Brunner packed his bag with blank sheets of manuscript paper, grabbed his typewriter, flew off to the Isle of Man, and locked himself in an hotel room. Ten, or eleven, or twelve days later, he reappeared, bleary-eyed from shortage of sleep, clutching the finished manuscript, which in a few months would be dazzling his growing reading audience with its clarity, feeling, knowledgeability, and depth of understanding of life and the world.

Reading the foregoing account of a "driven" writer at work makes one feel pretty grim, doesn't it? If *that* is what it takes, you may say to yourself—boy! then there's no hope for the average person.

Most Compulsive Assignments Not for Money

Alas, the method by which Brunner gets his inspiration from an unknown drive inside him more often produces failure, moneywise, than success. Here's an example:

Some years ago, I was at a friend's house late one night. Staying with him at the time was his younger brother, a youth who had a lackluster appearance and who was always tired. Shortly before midnight said younger brother wandered in from the kitchen and announced that he was deadbeat and was going to bed. Before he could depart the phone rang; the call was for him. The person at the other end was in a state of boisterous enthusiasm and his voice projected to where I sat: "Dave," he boomed cheerfully, "we're having a party, and it's the greatest. Come on over."

All of us have seen happen what I saw then, and possibly have even experienced it ourselves. Before the eyes of his older brother and myself, Dave *changed*. The dead-beat look vanished. As if by magic, his appearance of extreme exhaustion disappeared and there, standing before us, was a normal, healthy, high-energy young man. He went to the party, naturally. After he had excitedly gone his way, his older brother said to me sourly, "No time or energy to look for work, or earn a living on his own, but lots of time for parties. And he really is the life of the party wherever he goes. He won't be home until morning." He shook his head, sadly.

You'll agree, the same intensity of energy was triggered in this young man as Brunner reported to me. But in David's case it led downhill all the way. His inner assignments directed him towards frivolity, not money.

Of the people who receive their assignments from some chance triggering of energy within them, for every John Brunner there are hundreds of David variations, who, if they stay out of jail, eventually end up in Group One, where someone tells them what to do (gives them assignments) eight hours a day.

Receiving and Accepting Assignments Is Normal

In regard to this, a clarification is in order: It is not wrong to receive assignments. For 99% of the population in Capitalist countries, and 100% in Communist countries, this is the way people get started.

The average person coming up to adulthood seldom knows what he wants to do. Often he gets his first job by happenstance. In such a job, he is given—usually—a low level (and low pay) assignment.

A first assignment constitutes a guideline for a newcomer to the marketplace. It points a direction for him, and teaches him lessons out of life situations. It also gives him his first chance to adjust to the shock of working eight or more hours a day.

Since our newcomer is a human being, and has that great human brain, he is already—if he is ambitious—looking over the business world and evaluating his prospects.

Each day, his work assignment consists of a series of exactly defined tasks quite different from the vague thinking he did before he got the job. Perhaps most important, usually what he does for one employer is similar to what is required by other employers.

So his first job, with its assignments, can be a learning experience of great value despite the low pay that is initially involved. In fact, assignments from other people occasionally help even very able persons to improve their abilities. A good example to illustrate this is also from the field of professional writing. But happily this time it is from one of the fabulous branches of the writing business.

The TV and Film Assignment System

Hollywood has taught many writers lessons in productivity. One man I know who had written by self-assignment 128 separate short stories and novelettes and eight novels in a 22-year magazine, paperback, and book career, came to Hollywood a while back. In the next six years he wrote over 400 half-hour and hour scripts for television, and several motion picture screenplays, all on assignments from movie or TV producers.

As a comparison, an hour TV show is the equivalent of a novella (a good half novel). A half-hour script compares to a long short story or a novelette.

What had happened?

Well, Hollywood has a system. The writer must train himself to prepare an outline. That is, he must know in advance, before writing it in detail, what a story will be about, how it develops, how it ends. He communicates these elements to the producer, or story editor, in an interview. If his summary is approved, he is then given the assignment to write the outline of what he has until now only described verbally. Preferably such outlines run from six to ten pages.

If the written outline is approved, then the writer usually is given the assignment to write the first draft of the script. If the first draft is approved, he is assigned to write the finished script. In each of these steps, he is paid an agreed-upon contractual amount—paid for the outline, paid for the first draft, and additionally paid for the finished script.

Those writers who can fit into the assignment system, as did my acquaintance, often earn huge incomes from TV and the movies.

(Incidentally, so far as I know, the foregoing account is the first time the Hollywood method has ever been described in print. For some reason, TV writers have been extremely secretive about it. Over the years I knew a number of script writers. Not once did any one of them tell me what I have just told you. Potential TV writers take note. You have your agent contact the producer and convince him that you won't waste his time. It's much simpler for him to deal with writers whom he knows from their past performance. But still, hip people with certain types of personality—the twelve qualities—do break in.)

But now—my point.

The writer whom I have been discussing, when he assigned writing tasks to himself, produced a strictly limited total of published (the equivalent of performed) work. But when he did his writing by assignment from someone else—ah! what a difference in overall output!

Please note also: In writing for television, he continued to do a similar kind of work to that which he had chosen for himself in his youth. So not every person who receives assignments is doing labor of no interest to himself. In fact, as many millions of individuals work at congenial occupations as at non-congenial ones, and good-naturedly accept assignments within their frame of training and interest.

So now, having said this much, we can come to the fundamental idea of Quality Two.

Measure Your Ability to Accept an Assignment

What is the highest level assignment you can accept? (That you will actually perform, that is.)

Can you accept an assignment from yourself? Or do you need a clear-cut company heirarchy system whereby your immediate superior is recognized by you as an authorized-to-give-you-an-assignment person? For such an authorized individual, and *his* superiors, you can agree to perform, and will perform, certain tasks within the narrow dynamics of the company's activities.

Could you accept an order from the President of the United States when, for example, he sends his Greetings to you on your 18th birthday? Some young men, anticipating that they were destined to go to Viet Nam, wouldn't. They left the country rather than accept that assignment.

How about the Income Tax Department? Thirteen per cent of Americans pay no, or little, income tax. They have never filed. They refuse to "play that crazy game," as one man put it to me.

At his peak income time, this individual operated as a croupier in Las Vegas under one or another of the several assumed names he had adopted, and spent time building a background for, while still quite young.

He could accept the exhilarating atmosphere of the gambling world, and the fact that his employers withheld taxes on his behalf was not a problem to him. His salary was what was left. That's all he was concerned with. As a croupier he had some little private method of making extra cash that he was very mysterious about, but of course no taxes were paid on that.

In his down-and-out periods, he was willing to wash dishes in a restaurant, drive a small delivery truck, work in a filling station, be a parking lot attendant, and act as a gun-carrying guard at special sales night at a department store.

So there really is an assignment level for almost everybody— something they *will* do either on a self-assignment basis or for payment from some other person.

Measure Your Ability to Give an Assignment

Basic question two: Whom can *you* give an order (assignment) to, really? By really I mean something that they then actually do.

Can you get your own son to do something? Your wife? If so, do you have to threaten them? If these questions seem blunt, they are—because we're trying to find out for you what you can do in terms of assignments.

Using a wife or a son as examples may be unfair. Some top executives these days can't get anything more than insults from their drop-out heir.

Here's what I'm coming to:

If you can only accept an assignment from a hash joint owner, do it—but notice it.

If your level is a clerk in a grocery store—notice that.

Start where you are.

The question naturally arises, how did human beings—those two-legged creatures with the big brains—ever get to a level of inner something where they work under orders either at jobs they don't like or which don't pay enough?

Another question: Why can't you simply decide that you are going to give yourself a moneymaking assignment? The consequences of a successful assignment on the big-money level has made it possible for some men to become millionaires (starting at zero income) before they are thirty.

Why not you?—you may ask.

To answer that we need to examine the underlying dynamics of who and what can get an assignment and at what level—and why or why not with money attached.

Moving Yourself Up the "Assignment Ladder"

Look! A frightened person.

There he goes. He's hurrying away—evading, withdrawing.

The action of fear is retreat, and there are many ways of retreat.

The salesman who goes to a movie instead of following up a lead is evading—the evasion, the retreat, of fear. The speaker who excuses himself a few minutes before he is due to say a few words; the man who wants a raise but keeps putting off contacting the boss; the girl who crosses a street to avoid a young man . . .

Actions of fear.

The person who sits at home when he should be out confronting the world, competing, fighting for his share of its goods, is not just withdrawing any more. He is in a chronic state of withdrawal.

This also applies to the person who has got himself a low-pay niche. By limiting the area where he competes he maintains a precarious peace of mind, but the price is high: failure.

So much—for the moment—for the action of fear.

Anger: the Emotion That Produces Both Low and High Assignments

Observe the angry man! His fists are clenched. His face is flushed. His mind is made up. He goes forward.

It is the forward motion of attack.

Angry people can have a lot of drive. They can get things done. Since they are better at this than fear people, they are often in positions of control and direction.

Even the most psychotic anger can sometimes achieve great effects, so receptive is the world to *any* forward-going action. Hitler's rages terrorized even his generals who were not otherwise frightened under the most severe gunfire. Khrushchev, when he was the Russian leader, displayed enough anger wherever he went to create the image of a very dangerous man.

In the U.S. we used to have large numbers of what might be called big, mad, successful business men. There is reason to believe that fewer such persons are now around. Anger is less and less an acceptable emotion in this country, and so there has been a gradual evolution towards greater self-control.

However, expression of anger still has its place. This is because when a person attacks something successfully he immediately feels better. Noting this, psychologists have determined that the individual who becomes angry achieves release of tension when he gives vent to his rage by attacking the object of it.

The action of rage, therefore, is a going forward to attack.

So much for the action of rage at this time.

The Best Assignments Go to Him Who Can Be Straightforward

Watch two people together, conversing in a warm, intimate fashion. One reaches forward, taps the other on the shoulder to make a point. The other laughs and squeezes his companion's hand gently. Then they walk off, arm in arm.

The action of friendship is going forward to envelope and enfold. To be a part of.

The embrace of lovers, the congeniality of friends, a group gathering, a community sing, a Kiwanis luncheon, the friendly discussion of and solution of a problem, a cooperative endeavor in which the participants engage spontaneously, any joining together for a friendly purpose—these are the actions of good fellowship and love.

They are going-toward actions, not to attack but to-be-one-with.

In business, a person who is like this is straightforward. He levels with you in a high-energy fashion. The anger person engages in something which seems similar to this, but his "candor" takes the form of giving you some dark "truths" about yourself. It is not that he isn't often a good observer, but there is a destructive darkness in him. Eventually you should learn to notice the difference between good straightforward advice from a person who means well by you, and from the critic who has a need to hit at you and others.

It is believed by at least one school of psychologists that all physical actions are some variation or combination of withdrawal, going against, and going toward.

I list them here because they are interesting concepts, and undoubtedly have some truth in them.

They do give a vivid picture, you'll agree.

Apathy Receives the Lowest Level Assignments

But I want to add one more: apathy.

Baby, child, teen is sick. While ill, baby, etc., goes into apathy. Baby, etc.'s body learns what apathy is.

(I know of no exceptions; do you? Everybody has been severely sick at least once in his lifetime.)

We see in later years people remembering in their body *in*-actions what they learned when they were in apathy. The motion of the environment goes around them, perhaps even through them, almost unnoticed.

Such people are holding still in a limp way. Other people move them around, hold their arms and guide them across a street, or lead them to a desk and say, "Do this!"

Apathy, of course, is given low-level assignments—in work and in competition. But Apathy has the same kind of giant brain as any other human being. And if you, Apathy, are reading this—read on. This world is for you, also.

Yes, Apathy can have and can keep money. Apathy, shown a way out and up, can find the pathway and climb.

Different Emotional States: Different Assignments

We don't have to be trained psychologists to know that each of these actions (as well as the inaction of apathy) ordinarily leads the person who is possessed by one or another to different types of occupations.

Anger is given a different assignment from that acceptable to Fear.

And Camaraderie is assigned what neither Fear nor Anger can achieve.

Out of the melange of feeling and consequent physical action that I have been describing has come the assignment status you are presently, rigidly, in.

What to do about it?

Notice it. Notice exactly what assignment level you can accept and from whom. Does your automatic assignment level lead to money? If yes, hold onto it. If no, notice *that*. We're beginning to get a clearer picture, aren't we?

Does this mean we are doomed to our individual lot? No.

Is there anything we should do about these emotions? No, not really. (Although the Anger person could learn a little more restraint.)

Why not do something?

Because all a grown-up needs is a direction.

Look! A person who suddenly sees a pathway. There he goes—up the side of the cliff.

The action of *knowing what to do* is forward and upward.
A few more words need to be said about assignments.

The Naturals: Who Can Already Give Assignments

Let's for a moment do a switch and look at this whole idea from
the viewpoint of a very special type of person—who also exists
in this country by the millions. I refer to that estimable character,
a man who early showed "leadership" qualities, and veritable
legions of whom live in the fine homes of America. I refer to your
employer or the esteemed head of your department.

All over the U.S.A. (and of course in other countries) he is the
man who hands out assignments. Being astute in his own fashion,
he discovers by an employee's reactions and appearance what kind
of assignments he will accept.

THE ASSIGNMENT SCALE

—Joe (Joe Smith, of course), sweep the floor
—Joe, your job each morning is to unlock the door and air the
  place out (or turn the heat up).
—Joe, be a good fellow and make the guys some coffee, will
  you?

*[A couple of levels here where Joe knows what his work is, and
he cannot be detoured to do errands.]*

—Joe, I want you to sit on this phone until you get a yes or
  no answer—
—Joe, ride herd on this order, and see it through the plant,
  will you?
—Mr. Smith, could I trouble you to come into my office for
  a discussion about a project I'd like you to undertake?
—Mr. Smith, at your convenience any time this afternoon, will
  you have your secretary contact my secretary and arrange
  for us to get together before dinner? We have to start thinking about setting up a new program for the Jenkins account.

Which last is just about as courteous an assignment as a man can hope for. The previous ones were gradational from downright blunt commands up towards greater politeness.

In the way an employer or a straw boss gives you assignments, you can detect—if you don't have your ego up as a barrier to good sense and good observation—which category of chronic emotional state you are probably in. Are you Apathy, or Fear, or Anger, or Straightforward? He notices automatically, and in a general way—depending on his personality—he takes advantage.

So don't wait with bated, hopeful breath for some millenium to change human nature. Make your own adjustments now.

The reason for your employer's behavior is that it's not as easy to be a boss as you might think. The man who can hand out assignments has to have a hitherto unknown (unknown until these twelve qualities were observed) inner resource for the role; or else, by studying other capable persons, he acquired knowledge about a certain line of work, braced himself, and made himself into a capable person, also.

Paying a Salary Is Not Enough

Looked at from a remote vantage point, it might appear that the simplest way to get people to work on your behalf is to pay them a salary.

I have some unhappy information for you, if you think that is all there is to it. Unless you have some of the twelve qualities I am here describing you will not be able to get a day's work out of a paid employee. You see, employees also are astute in their fashion. They quickly discover when an employer isn't up to it. Soon, in such a business, no one is working but the boss—except, of course, in some abysmally limited way.

And this is as true on a collective farm in Red China as it is in a restaurant on any Main Street in America.

How can such a cruel thing be so?

That was, in effect, the question a man named George asked me some years ago. He had always believed that certain successful men in his area had either inherited their business or had managed by some crookery to get hold of one; and he felt furthermore that their arbitrary behavior in relation to their employees was unnecessary. Finally, he had borrowed money from his wife's relatives, set up a print shop, and hired three assistants to help him operate it.

And they didn't do anything.

What went wrong?, George wanted to know.

Well—employees don't accept assignments from people like George. Not *won't,* but *don't.* George was not the type. He didn't have the one applicable to that situation of the twelve qualities.

To see what's wrong, let's do what Descartes, the French philosopher, recommended in his "Rules for the Direction of the Mind." Descartes' rule: Examine a problem in minute detail.

By this means we observe in George's approach to being a business man and a boss one illuminating fact: somehow, he was doing most of the work himself.

Pin that down. It showed a wonderful potentiality. George was trying to succeed. He had given himself an assignment, and he at least was working to make it happen.

That's where George should have started.

If I had caught him in time, I'd have told him to tell his wife to fire the three non-working assistants. When I mentioned that to him he said that he did finally, reluctantly, ask his wife to do this, but that the first employee she spoke to refused to accept her discharge. His attitude: *"He* hired me"—meaning George; "I'll accept my discharge notice only from him"—meaning from George.

How could such a thing happen? Well, it can. As soon as you inquire around you discover that there is a type of employee who senses "leadership" weakness with an intensity that he should be applying to his own success.

What finally happened was that George's money ran out, at which time he was able to "fire" the men himself—from a sort of a begging (that is, a victim) position. Being curious about such matters, I discovered that each recalcitrant employee had walked out of the bankrupt shop without a backward glance, and apparently with never a thought of his own contribution to the disaster.

The Georges of this world, if they go into business, should do so without employees—until they develop the ability to give an assignment that sticks.

Giving an Assignment to Your Victimizer

In the assignment department, we have of course the victimizer going full blast.

He has an advertisement in the paper or in the yellow pages, stating that he builds shelving. You call him, and he agrees to do the job, and extracts either full or part payment in advance. The weeks go by, and he cannot seem to get over to your place to build those shelves.

Reason is, his phone rings steadily with new assignments—on each of which he collects payment in advance in full or part. It is hard for him to find time to do the work.

The commercial world swarms with victimizers who accept assignments, knowing that they can't possibly fulfill the obligation at the time stated.

How do you become a non-victim in relation to such persons?

Go by the recommendation of a friend. In asking for and receiving such a recommendation, be sure to mention the points I have named. Find out how long it took before the job was done. People tend to forget.

Then ask the workman the exact starting date, and make the advance payment zero, or very small.

The assignment principle as such is not tarnished by the existence of these victimizers. Its purpose is to point a direction. Even as he is avoiding doing your job, the victimizer knows *where* he should be—over at your place doing the work for which he has been paid.

If you persist, the majority of them eventually show up.

In all instances where you give an assignment, the principle will work better if you are also a non-victim.

These twelve qualities do a lot of interlocking.

NOTE: *Straightforwardness does not mean that you reveal business secrets to any but authorized associates and personnel.*

3

Third Quality of the Money Personality: Developing an Automatic Profit Response

The money personality always has a personal, special reason for charging a profit.

The oldest of the three now successful men whose backgrounds I studied in order to write this book was a champion ballroom dancer in his teens; the first prize he ever won was a pair of fancy pajamas. It is what he did in relation to the pajamas that is significant. At the time he first told me the story, I asked him what he thought they were worth. "Oh," he said, "ten dollars."

A few weeks later I was surprised and amused to hear him tell a friend that he had won a pair of pajamas "worth twelve dollars and fifty cents."

A year went by. He did not wear the pajamas. They remained in their original carton, pristine pure. Then one day he referred to them as being worth fifteen dollars.

I was even then capable of having ironic thoughts about such odd revelations of character. And never gave the matter another thought until one day the youngest of the three men—Mr. C. —sold a well-used bedroom set for more than he paid for it.

This would not have impressed me so much if it weren't for the fact that a short time before I had sold *my* bedroom furniture for about 15% of what I had paid for it, and it was much newer.

At the time of these two events, so ordinary and normally the kind of thing that is completely unnoticed when one investigates human behavior, I did not of course realize that I had witnessed a key mental mechanism at work. But not too many moons ago, when I finally put these and other observations under the bright light of inductive logic, I had another quality for the person who can accumulate the stuff.

Upgrading Value Is a Trait You Must Cultivate

Both these men unconsciously did an upgrading job on value by an automatic process. What is new about this is that, by my observation, part of the process is unconscious. In a world where everybody knows about the profit motive, the rake-off, the seller's percentage, what nobody has noticed until I perceived it is that only people who can do this deep in their heads, automatically, without thinking, have to date been able to get in on the act.

If you do not have this ability, you will most likely not be able to raise the price at all. But if you have tried by various devious methods—by mail, by bracing yourself after a tongue lashing from your wife—you probably have discovered by now that it really isn't bringing you any money.

Often, people will think you're cheating: there's something about you that doesn't seem right. And so they hasten to buy a similar item from a victimizer who really cheats them but who simultaneously gives them a feeling that they have got something of value because he has an automatic value-creating mechanism in his head.

To Each His Own Profit Reason

Every well-to-do person that I talked to, or read about, had a reason for why he is entitled to put up the price. These reasons vary from one person to another.

One man I know guarantees his work and fulfills his guarantee. Thus he justifies his rather large mark-up. Another man has convinced himself that he saves his customers money. (Sometimes he does.) A third feels that his reasoning ability is a jewel of great price and that he can charge what the traffic will bear. A fourth feels that the laborer is worthy of his hire.

J. Paul Getty, one of the world's wealthiest men, wrote in a recent *Playboy* article that wealth must serve a constructive purpose. When I read that, I realized I was being given *his* reason.

But when I told Getty's idea to a man who owns a factory which manufactures fine instruments, he said scathingly: "That's phony!" *His* reason for charging a profit on his factory's output is "quality of product."

I have found that people who can make or keep money do not believe in each other's reasons. This would seem to indicate that the reason is very important and personal, reflecting perhaps some early traumatic experience.

Whatever the reason, until now it's all been done automatically in each person's head, and has been unnoticed as being a necessary part of the moneymaking faculty.

Unusual Profit Reasons

Some of the reasons do not at first sight seem applicable. For example, a short time ago I read an article about Alfred Hitchcock, the TV and movie director. In it he was quoted as saying that money meant nothing to him.

As I considered that statement, I conjured a mental picture of Hitchcock. What I recalled validated my instantaneous feeling that the only postures I have ever seen him in were designed to make him money.

The author of the article goes on to describe Mr. Hitchcock's sumptuous home and his wine cellar with its $50,000 worth of fine and rare wines, of which the owner was exceedingly and properly proud. But it takes money to own such treasures.

In considering all this, I was presently able to push aside my old-style reactions to Mr. Hitchcock's easy dismissal of the value of money. I remembered that the original Henry Ford said money meant nothing.

Since Henry Ford I had taken the trouble to accumulate two billion dollars, it became apparent that somehow, by believing money means nothing, that inner switch for jacking up the price has a free swing to it. And so Henry Ford's and Alfred Hitchcock's reason for charging plenty has to be included among the better "reasons."

Of course, I deduce what these people mean. They mean that a person should concentrate on doing something basically worthy, and money will flow to him. It is interesting to note that there are worthy actions which do not produce money, so the question of what motivated Hitchcock and Henry Ford to concentrate on actions that do produce the cash flow, could well be a subject for further study

One more point in this connection: If you are a person who has no money, who believes that money means nothing, and it's not a failure pose—then this is not your problem. One or more of the other qualities, other than the ability to upgrade value, will be what you need to deal with.

A. P. Giannini, the founder of the Bank of America, said that wealth must serve the community and help it prosper or it isn't worth anything.

We may see that he also had in his head an automatic justifier for making a profit, and—as we know—a good one.

Reasons for Profit Making Deserve Respect

Whenever I hear of or read these reasons these days, I have a different feeling about them than I used to. It is a feeling of respect. Is the ability to upgrade value worthy of respect?

At first sight, it would seem doubtful. The world is so full of chiselers and money gougers that we tend not to notice that underlying a lot of the swindling, may actually be an ability. Possibly we need to learn to separate the ability from the swindling philosophy that many people have acquired in the university of life.

They learned the wrong lessons. Unknown to them, they had the real key, a natural talent for upgrading value. All the rest is their own foolishness.

I feel that a person who can upgrade value has a basically good feeling about things and objects, particularly. The old rag picker salvages what has no value for the housewife. The eyes of the upgrader of value look around the world and in some areas at least see substance and meaning where you and I see nothing.

I would surmise that people who do not have this automatic ability to upgrade value cannot participate in the profit system, except as pawns. It could be that guilt is involved. Most people seek money only where the ownership is not in question, and they do so by acceptable or justified methods. The least guilty place to be is on a salary.

You see how that is. A salary is paid by agreement between you and the person who pays it. You can be pretty sure that if he actually agrees, then he's probably paying you less than you're worth. Hence, you feel completely secure in accepting what he gives.

Select a Suitable Stage for Your Profit Act

Probably the best place to make money is on a stage of your own creation. You need a location where you can receive money for an acceptable service or object. If you set your stage correctly, then you will have a proper public image. An illusion is created and maintained whereby the buyer of your product automatically accepts your right to be the go-between on the deal.

The best stage is a store, an office, or a business. If you can also convey to your buyer that you have been there a long time, so much the better.

But the stage, though always necessary in some form, only makes it easier. It is not the decisive factor. The person at the center of the stage has to have the ability to upgrade value inside his own skin or he'll soon have an empty, bankrupt stage.

If the ability to make money was merely a science, then the Capitalist system could not long survive. Everybody with a grain of sense in him would quickly learn the methods and the economy would level out.

I suggest to all interested persons that what I have said, and am saying, is as close to a science as the average person will ever get.

In analyzing the various reasons for charging a profit that successful people have given me, or that I have read about, I discover that they break down into four main types:

BASIC PROFIT REASONS

1. They're helping.
2. They're delivering quality.
3. They provide a useful service.
4. They have a worthwhile vision, an ideal, for which they now or at some later time will need large sums.

RULE FOR ACHIEVING QUALITY THREE

Select one, and only one of these reasons, write it on a card, carry that card with you, and look at it many times each day as a reminder.

Select a Profit Reason That Suits You

Don't be an idiot and choose a method that doesn't fit your character. If in life you're a taker and not a giver, then put out a quality product or do a useful service. But if you're one of those people who are always doing odd jobs for the neighbors, think how much more help you could give the world if you had money.

I'm serious. Many a person justifies his mark-up to himself because of all the people he's supporting with his money. If you have such a reason, don't tell anyone; just do it, be aware that you're doing it, and keep your own counsel.

Select Only a Successful Reason

A word of warning. If you have a specific variation of one of the four principal types, be sure that the method you write down on your card under the heading "Rule Two" is actually that of a person who is successful, moneywise.

I voice this caution because one person to whom I told this portion of my idea promptly gave me *his* reason. It seemed quite a good one; but afterwards I remembered that he had given a mutual friend a small check on a purchase and had asked him to wait three days before depositing the check.

A man who has so little money should not instantly volunteer his reason—but he did. Like me, he was only a cat; yet I watched the money scene for nearly five years before arriving at my conclusions, and I still felt qualified only to look at and observe a king. I judged my situation on the simple, pragmatic basis that I had no money. He, who also had none, nevertheless pretended to be one of the kings. Possibly charging a profit is not his problem. Not improbably we need to look to another quality for what ails his bank account. But it is also true that some people's egos impel them to blithely offer suggestions in areas where they are not qualified. You've got to watch out for such usurpers—if you want to make money.

And so, I have now told you that being able to charge a profit is a fairly rare human quality in our society, or any other. The great majority of people either cannot do it at all or can do it only on a gradient scale.

The quality can be acquired. But it had first to be observed as something that is of the person and not of the system.

Remember, the money personality requires that every commercial transaction show some kind of a profit.

It is possible that Huntington Hartford, the A and P heir, suffered the most dramatic losses experienced by any one person in recent times. HH is reported to have inherited one hundred million dollars, and to have lost eighty million of it in a few years. Not too long ago, in a television interview HH gave a detailed explanation for his losses. But we need not concern ourselves with these numerous itemized accounts of where the money went. Even medical doctors only make about a million dollars in a lifetime of work; the rest of us much less. So when a man can lose *eighty* million in eight years, something is wrong.

Was he a victim? He still has money, so if he was a victim it was only up to a point. A real victim could not have stopped anywhere on the road down. Did he suffer from an inability to charge a profit? At first look, that would seem to be an irrelevant question. This young man had enough wealth to keep a hundred people in absolute luxury for a hundred years.

Huntington Hartford Lacked Profit Reason

Yet we may surmise that when someone came to HH with an appeal for funds for a worthy enterprise, our heir failed to ask a vital profit-oriented, though not necessarily profit-making, question. The question: "Since I am not concerned with making money, all I want to know is, how can I do what you want without suffering a loss, and who will see to it that I don't lose?"

He could even have said, "If I could be assured that I would not lose more than a million dollars a year for the rest of my life in my various contributions to art, literature, theater, and charities, I'd be glad to underwrite this worthy cause. Can you assure me of this, and, if you can't, is there someone who will be associated with the enterprise who can?"

It was that simple. But he didn't ask that question. Or, if he did, it was just talk. He didn't mean it at the gut level where you hold onto money (keep past profits) and mean what you say.

Would his hearers have despised HH for such a defensive question? Would they have thought, "Boy! what kind of a vulture is this?" In short, would it have made him sound like a victimizer?

Not if they had in a rational way the twelve qualities I am describing, or if they were in other ways genuinely people of good will. Sensible people understand that the well-intentioned among the wealthy help causes and not individuals—except for small handouts. But the world still swarms with subjective characters like the one who tried to borrow money from Mr. C. on an unbusinesslike basis to start his own business.

Undoubtedly, such people approach Huntington Hartford in much greater numbers, and I can tell you that their attitude is: "Why shouldn't he loan me the money? He has so much he won't miss it!" In the course of my study, I talked to these types and asked their justification. Each had essentially the same impatient attitude, and felt that it was a lousy world if a guy that had it didn't share it.

In this book we are not concerned with basic issues such as what is the best economic and political system. The twelve qualities —including automatic profit response—are absolute necessities for success in every system now in existence.

As I see it, it is unlikely that our present system will be overthrown in the visible future. So this is the one we have to get along with and in.

I have special advice for non-conformists later in the book.

Learn to Accept the Need for Profit

People who cannot charge a profit show it in many ways. Recently I was introduced to a former car salesman, who made the statement that automobiles were too high-priced. He informed me that when he had been an auto salesman his reason for his poor sales performance was that the firm was overcharging for its machines. Why not—he had repeatedly asked the owner of the agency—take a little less profit, and sell a few more cars to make up the difference? Thus the pressure would be off and selling would be easier.

One day, this young salesman found that his name was not listed on the salesman's board.

Was he right? Was there something to his complaint? Was this why he was not able to sell cars?

He was wrong. His complaint was not well-founded. His employer's price was in line with the competition. So his own inability to sell more than an occasional car had nothing to do with the price being asked.

But now, the other, automatic profit response side.

At the beginning of his career, Mr. C., one of the now rich men I knew when I was younger, seldom made more than ten thousand a year. At one time, he was a salesman of mutual funds, which have a fixed charge from which those selling and promoting them must receive their income. Mr. C., noting that the percentage involved would be considered reasonable by the average buyer, decided to capitalize on the modest size of this charge.

At once he became a top mutual salesman. There were weeks on end when his income averaged $3500 *a day.*

Please note: The auto salesman had a basic resistance to profit taking. Mr. C., on the other hand, recognized its validity and actually sought a method of enlisting the buyer's support of the seller's profit.

Why? What was the factor that the auto salesman lacked that Mr. C. had. It was this: The auto salesman, lacking a reason within himself that justified his employer's mark-up, approached each prospect inwardly agreeing that the car wasn't worth the price that was being asked. Mr. C., however, had early convinced himself that his share of the profit was ridiculously low.

Socializing Not a Substitute for Profit Reason

There are numberless people in this wide world who are in the peculiar state of not being able to accept a successful outcome. They appear to have a deep, dark, inner negation which impels them to screw things up.

One long-time salesman reported taking along on his route a neophyte hired by his company. On several occasions, just at the key moment when an order was about to be consummated (i.e., a sale made), the new man actually stepped between the veteran salesman and the prospect and diverted the latter's attention, changing the conversation (which was of course strictly business up to that moment) over to sports.

At the end of that day, the veteran discovered that he had achieved his lowest sales total in twenty years on the road.

> The more important your prospect, the less time he has for interviews and chitchat. Stick to the business between you, using a systematic approach (which your company or your experience, let's hope, has taught you) and leave repartee for cocktails, parties, and such. Sometimes a buyer is in an expansive mood, or else takes a fancy to the seller. He may, *after*

the business is concluded, invite the latter out for a drink, at which point the conversation may move to more personal matters. Some salesmen pride themselves on their socializing technique. These men need to ask themselves how much they are really making.

The non-achiever described in the foregoing account lacks the ability to charge a profit, so he cannot permit *any* profitable transaction to be completed in his presence. We may also speculate that business matters are not real to him (see Quality Eight) and so he acts as if they're not real to anyone else either.

On Placing Value

The money personality places a value on at least one person in this world: himself.

How can you decide that you have value and are entitled to ask a profit? For that is what having a reason implies: placing a positive valuation on yourself. Perhaps I can encourage you to become an optimistic self-evaluator.

To start, you have a big boost from the good old U.S.A. You will share in the growth of America and will have *that* value as a gift from your country.

Need proof of such value and that it is growing?

Just imagine how it would be if every working man, or in fact anyone whether he was willing to work or not, could always receive $100 a month. That was the ultimate dream of one idealist during the Great Depression of the Thirties. He would capture an audience of one, two, three or more persons on the street or in a building and with great emotion expound his dream of the millenium.

"If necessary we must have a revolution," he said, "and overthrow the government to achieve so great a goal."

Today we give $100 or more a month to most pensioners in progressive states. And we don't ask too many questions about other sources of income they may have.

A sum approximating $100 a month has become a casual figure

which many states give an unemployed workman who is looking for another job. If he cannot find one, if his unemployment aid expires and he has to seek Welfare assistance, the County or City Aid Service will furnish him with the equivalent of $100 a month until he finds a job, or they find one for him.

The Utopian dream of one man, for which he urged the shedding of blood, if necessary, has been the incidental achievement available to the poorest man in the land.

What happened? In 15 years, from mid-Depression to the Fifties, Americans moved up from a period where a dime was a treasured coin to the beginnings of our present prosperity. There was a year in the Thirties when the entire national income of 150 million Americans was $34 billion. A decade and a half later it was ten times that. Now it is much greater and has passed the trillion mark.

Can conditions improve? They certainly can.

Can you participate in the improvement of the national economy? You did.

So—what's the problem? Why not just sit back and wait for America the Bountiful to deliver this delightful prosperity to your door?

Well, you can do exactly that—if you want only the minimum to be deposited to your account. The big money, however, is going to people who have a goodly supply of Quality Three—automatic profit response.

The Master Salesman, whom I mentioned in Section One, told me many interesting stories out of his life as a sales manager and sales promotion executive.

Increased Profit a Psychological Hazard

One example: A group of salesmen making between $500 and $600 dollars a week for the first time in their lives began to talk as if their good fortune couldn't possibly continue. They had to be given special training courses to prevent them from quitting their jobs and finding something in which they could feel more secure.

These salesmen lacked an automatic profit response in relation to making more money. Investigation established that they were suffering from salesman's remorse—guilt—on the larger amount of money which they were obtaining from the buyer.

Re-training consisted essentially of convincing them of the changing values in a changing world, of proving to them that in that same changing economy the buyer's purchase—in this instance of California real estate—would eventually turn out to be the best investment the buyer had ever made. It was.

Yet, at some deep level these salesmen kept thinking that old ways and old prices would go on in some similar though negative fashion. Or that, if things did change, the old, lesser ways would sneak back when no one was looking, and take over once more.

Never, never again *then,* and never, never again *now!*

What the experience of these salesman tells us is that some reasons for profit-taking are better than other reasons. So, in choosing your reason, why not devise one that doesn't have to be changed when you suddenly find yourself making more money.

Think I'm joking? You'll learn the hard way, when it happens —if you don't take it into account now.

Some Realities of Your Reason for Profit Taking

Your reason for asking a profit is part of your public image.

One more thought about this: It is inadvisable to complain to your customers about how high your overhead is—or how much your last illness cost—or the legal costs of collecting money owed you—or how much you had to loan to your brother-in-law.

Such reasons may get you a little sympathetic business, but it may lose you a better class of customer that doesn't care to hear sad songs.

We may analyze that people with a strong need for sympathy grew up in a twisted environment where it paid to pretend to be a victim. In most U.S. cities such pretense is no longer necessary.

Which tells us there has already been progress. People have already changed for the better. They can do more, have more, than they once could. They will not take kindly to reverses. It will not be easy to turn the clock back on them. They will reject old-style images.

Individually and economically man is greater than he was. Everywhere is evidence of new *think* and new *do.*

Athletic records continue to tumble. In every field there is more sophistication, more knowledge, and more understanding.

Basic scientific discoveries have been made so rapidly in recent years that invention has for some time now not been able to keep pace. As a result a new era of opportunity is dawning for the technically minded. Bright young people who probably have to have a modicum of scientific training will for some years still be able to fit together various discoveries *which have already been made* into stunning new combinations.

Scientifically, mechanically, technologically, the civilized world is about to take another giant step into the future.

On Asking a Profit

This is about a man who couldn't. (His story sums up Quality Three.)

A woman who came to one of my lectures told me about her husband's used photographic equipment shop.

First wrong in it: It was extra dirty, messy.

Second wrong: He often bought outright junk. Some of the stuff was actually broken, worthless, and unsalable.

Third wrong: In buying, he played king and usually offered more than he should for the almost-trash. But often after a period of maintaining his self-esteem by spreading largesse, he would suddenly become stingy and with a take-it-or-leave-it attitude would offer a ridiculously low price for a choice item, fail to obtain it, and then afterwards she would discover from an un-chance word dropped by him that he blamed her.

The blame was based on the fact that, wife-like, she occasionally tried to restrain his spending sprees, which were really playing-the-big-shot madnesses. His blame claim: remembering her admonishments, he failed to bid high enough.

(I suspect the Freudians would have a thing or two to say about a man who somehow muffed the buying of salable items and instead filled his store with stuff that was seldom more than a short breath away from the junkpile.)

Fourth wrong: Periodically he would have a sale during which the junk would be priced at less than he had paid for it, on the principle that every "businessman" had sales to dispose of overstock. "At least," he informed his long-suffering spouse, "this way we get back a part of our original investment."

How did this man survive?

Prior to going into business for himself, he had been an employee in the piano repair department of a big organization. When, later, they were swamped with work, our hero would help out by carting several pianos to the rear of his own shop. There, aware of the standards of a going concern, and knowing that he had to do a first class repair job like any good employee, he did. But it was on the basis of being able to accept an assignment (Quality Two).

Thus, in his spare time, he earned a fair income, and his little family had food and a roof over their heads.

This man is an excellent example of a person who knew many of the motions of business but lacked the particular ability to buy or sell for profit. You can see that the whole operation, dirt and all, would have had a certain sanity to it if on every transaction there had actually been a 40% to 100% rake-off.

So, essentially, this man needed only to have had a personal reason for charging that profit.

But lacking that one quality, he should not be in his own business—yet. Not until, by carrying the little white card with his reason on it for jacking up the price, he can finally do so.

Friend—*carry that card!*

4

Fourth Quality of the Money Personality: Maintaining a High Energy Level

The money personality stays awake and alert all day long, using whatever stimulants he knows are suitable to him.

Your Energy Quotient

It takes legwork and armwork to go anywhere and do anything on this planet.

When we do this, we become progressively tired and lose our oomph, our zip, and our zoom.

Worse, as we observe people using their limbs, we notice that some move briskly all day and evening. Others are cocky enough in the morning but start slowing down in the afternoon. Still others are not good even in the morning, and by noon they're dragging and are definitely dead by night. Some, whenever seen, seem to be in a position of relative no-motion. This applies morning, afternoon, and evening.

For all we know, these latter persons have their moments for being as busy as anybody. But on occasion I have asked the acquaintances and relatives of some of these people: "Is he always like that?" Their answer—"Yes!"—could mean that these observers also missed him in those split seconds when he was moving. We might even speculate that he cannot sleep at night and so during the wee hours wanders about—in short, moves.

If so, it is very unlikely that his activities at such hours are financially rewarding.

My belief is that there are millions of non-movers who do not move because they are tired, and who sleep even longer at night than they do in the daytime.

If you are a non-mover or any other kind of dopey type (and I don't mean drugs), or know one about whom you are concerned, read these words just as long as you can keep your eyes open.

At this point I suspect that the horrified thought has already occurred to you that what I'm saying is that you're going to need some minimum amount of energy in order to make money. Anticipating this reaction on your part, my question to myself is this: How can I picture for you the energy that I have seen in some human beings? More important, how can I convince you that there is at least one way open to you whereby you can have a reasonable facsimile of such energy?

Examples of High Energy

I once watched Adlai Stevenson (the second time he was a presidential candidate) as he passed by. He was only a few feet away, and I could see him clearly. His face shone. His eyes were bright and gleaming. He walked with a firm, springy step.

He radiated good health and high-level energy. How high? You won't believe it until you experience a measureable duplicate of it yourself.

A while back I had business in Wichita, Kansas. I had a room in the Broad-something hotel. One day I entered the lobby—and stopped short. All the couches and settees and chairs were occupied by young men under thirty, with eyes that shone and faces that were bright and super-healthy.

Now, if you've ever been to Wichita and have seen its citizenry as they passed you in the street or spoke to you with their flat,

Middle-West voices, you'll have noticed that even those who are in good shape have a slowness about them. They seem to grow out of the prairie, and even at their best, which is shrewd, hard-working, and adequate, they look—

Nothing like what I saw in the lobby of that hotel. I was electrified. I made my way to the desk, and I whispered to the clerk, "Who are *those* men?"

They were the St. Louis Browns.*

I never did find out what the St. Louis National League baseball team was doing in Wichita. But they left me with a vivid memory that has lasted ever since, of a whole group of men in a condition of supreme physical well-being.

Having seen such splendid examples of the benefits of sports and exercise, was I motivated when I got home to go out into the backyard and do setting-up exercises? Nope. The truth is, exercise always made me feel tired quickly, so I didn't indulge.

I had been sitting down most of my life, and I could see no reason why I shouldn't continue in this pleasant, euphoric position: not thinking too much; occupied with intellectual matters; driving an old car; living in an old house with utility furniture; surviving from one story check to the next—barely.

Then one day somebody spoke to me, and I stood up. To my considerable surprise, I found I could move, also.

The person who addressed me was Mr. C., and what he said was that he had made a fortune since I had last seen him ten years before.

This stirred me into the activity that eventually led me to the ideas I am here describing to you, and to considerably greater affluence.

Why did I sit there all those years?

I had no place to go. The twelve pathways which I am now pointing out to you, didn't exist for me then. As soon as I became aware of them, I was off and running.

---

* The Browns later became the Baltimore Orioles, and moved from the National League to the American League.

The first thing for us all to face here is that the big companies which hire star athletes and groom them for top business leadership are most likely making a sound investment.

Healthy men think better and more clearly, and accomplish more.

Anger: Sometimes a Substitute for Good Health

Failing to achieve good health through exercise, we descend to the next natural level. This level has to do with—well, let's take a look.

Neurologists, using modern techniques, have located several control centers in the brain. There are, for example, perception centers, appraisal centers, feeling centers, and motor (action) centers.

The control centers with which we are immediately concerned are (1) the emotional center, (2) the intellectual center, and (3) the motor (action) center.

One of these is very likely acting as an automatic pilot for you. You—the pilot—are not actually in control at all.

If you are like your friends and neighbors, your conversation is most likely stereotyped, you are a creature of habit, and your thoughts are probably repetitious. Don't be fooled by over-intellectualization. All such behavior—whatever direction it takes—reflects the nature of the automatic condition, reflects which of these centers is the automatic pilot.

Now an automatic pilot is certainly a useful instrument for guiding a great ocean liner across to another land. But on a ship there is a clear differentiation between the robot pilot and the true pilot. If weather reports warn of a dangerous storm en route, or if the navigator desires to change course for any reason, the real pilot takes the helm until the automatic pilot can be re-set for the new course, or the danger is over.

In a human being no such obvious difference is observable between the true pilot and the automatic pilot.

The best way to explain this is to show you what this means in terms of behavior. First, a brief description of the three centers:

(1)   *The emotional center:* This is the heart of the creative will to win from which comes all desire and personal drive.

(2)   *The intellectual center:* This is the interpreter of communications where emotional needs are translated into conscious desires. The intellectual center receives messages from the emotional center, translates them into desires, makes plans for satisfying those desires, and issues orders to the motor center for action.

(3)   *The motor (action) center:* This is the center that gets things done. Desires and plans remain but fleeting figments of frustrating dreams unless the action center *executes* plans.

Now, recall what was said earlier about the basic going-against emotion of anger.

So there we have our next "natural."

Angry men, who have learned to smile, who have converted some of their rage into warmth, and have learned—as the saying goes—to get along with people (but, careful! don't cross them), are the second most actively doing people. In them, the true pilot is seldom in view; they are piloted by anger. But the limbs are flailing, and something is happening.

It has been estimated that 20% of the male population has this neurosis. Of these, about three-quarters—that is, 15% of the total male population—are off on some no-money madness of their own.

I have some pointed advice elsewhere in these pages for this 15%, the majority of whom have a quicker than average success potentiality.

By subtraction, we calculate that we have left about 5% of all the men in the country who, through anger, have been "driven" to achieve.

These angry men plus the men in Group One just about control the world, financially and otherwise. Is this morally right? The question is not valid within the frame of this book.

However, as I've already said, anger is a less acceptable emotion these days. People who accidentally have this emotion as their pilot more and more need to exercise restraint on quick rages. The true pilot needs to take charge oftener.

Many angry men exercise, or are impelled to play tennis or golf, etc., as a method of using up the adrenalin which they constantly pump into their bloodstreams. Thus, there is a certain amount of overlap between Energy Groups One and Two.

That just about completes our summation of the naturally successful people.

The Low-Activity People

Group Three consists of that largest-of-all total of individuals who have wrong-direction anger, or who are products of fear or apathy. A few of these people through some unusual circumstance can be successful in a society where you don't have to confront others directly. But the vast majority of them live ordinary, essentially unsuccessful lives.

We observed them a few chapters ago accepting varying assignments from employers. We may picture them sitting at desks doing routine tasks, standing at machines on eight-hour shifts, and otherwise waiting for a signal from a source of authority outside themselves to tell them what to do.

A small percentage of this type has got itself into a safe niche. Thus, away from stress, the person manages to straddle his day without over-fatigue, and in fact actually may smile and joke and seem to be in a good energy state.

These fortunate few are not headed anywhere in particular, money-wise. But as long as they remain in that safe niche without too much responsibility, and feel unthreatened, they *could* by careful investment build up a small estate.

Occasionally, such individuals misread their situation and decide to go into business for themselves. At which point the nightmare beginneth.

If you are a boss, and you have a good steady man whom you are considering for a top executive post, ask yourself two questions: (1) Does he exercise or engage in sport? (2) Is there *any* situation in which he can get angry at another person? If the answer to both questions is yes, and he is otherwise qualified, then he fits into one of the "natural" categories.

Should you accidentally put a fear type of person into a job that is "above" his inner acceptance, keep a sharp eye on him. He could grow, but more likely he will rapidly go to pieces.

Not too long ago, an acquaintance of mine, who was a member of a union, was asked by the union to sit on a board of arbitration. The task was completely outside of his reality, and he actually fell apart so completely that his wife had him committed to a VA hospital for mental patients.

If you observe in yourself withdrawal or fear tendencies, or a lot of apathy, but are in a variation of the stress-free low-level assignment situation that I have described, remain there for the moment. Let me later analyze what you must do. Meanwhile, finish reading this book.

Energy from Caffeine

The first heartening thing we notice about our Group Three people is that most of them have found a practical solution for getting through each workday. When I was in my teens, the older brother of an acquaintance of mine drank 26 bottles of Coca Cola each day. His reason: He could not, he reported, survive his ten-hour day in the store where he worked, without his "Coke" each 20 to 25 minutes.

What did he imbibe from the Coca Cola that enabled him to remain in motion? The answer: Coca Cola is about 35% caffeine—a stimulant. He could have achieved the same end-result with many cups of coffee or two caffeine tablets.

So, when during the day you see Apathy, Fear, and Misdirected Anger having another cup of coffee, you are observing people who have discovered a substitute for exercise. Don't despise the method. If, for some reason, you can't exercise, and if you're not naturally driven toward money by a controlled type of anger, this should also be your intermediate solution.

Ask your doctor what your substitute should be. Some people shouldn't take caffeine in any form, and other people are already overstimulated to a degree where additional stimulation is not the answer.

They're moving fast but toward the wrong goal. You've heard of the man who climbed on his horse and rode off in all directions. He belongs to this naturally overstimulated type. He is somehow not able to get with it. Maybe he needs to be calmed down.

That is just about all we need to observe about *normal* energy as we see it manifested in our energetic United States.

Other Drugs as a Source of Energy

A small number, percentage-wise, of Fears and Apathies, and particularly of Mis-directed Angers, have found that certain additional drugs seem to "turn them on."

Just in case you wonder—in this book we don't condemn anything that works. Frederick Faust, one of whose ten pseudonyms was Max Brand, sat down at his typewriter each morning with a quart of whiskey. By the time he finished the whiskey he had typed 14 manuscript pages on another of his hundreds of novels. By this method, his total annual production was about one and a half million words, the equivalent of 25 novels, and good ones they were, too.

Psychologists will tell you that liquor used in this fashion suppresses, or balances off, a deep neurosis; and you can usually tell the type by the fact that they don't get as drunk as might be expected from such an incredible dosage.

The things to notice about the use of liquor or drugs in connection with moneymaking, are:

First and foremost: is it actually a method that lifts you to the level of being a moneymaker?

Second and important: do you indulge privately and for the actual purpose of stimulating yourself to the useful production of a money-earning thing?

The word "privately" is important here. It tells us that you are not flaunting your unfortunate need because you are a rebel or because you are still trying to shock or "get even with" your parents or somebody else.

Don't misread "privately" to mean that there you and your congenial friends are revelling at a pot party in your apartment, and the police break in and arrest everybody. In such a situation, the narcotics squad is doing its duty as prescribed by law, and the pot party comes under the heading of a rebel action on your part.

If you're involved in drugs on that general level, notice it. You're an alienated person—a rebel. You have made the decision to be out of control of the establishment. I have some good money-making advice for you later on in this book.

Using Stimulants

So, what do I recommend?

Well, for myself, I finally figured out how I could exercise without becoming totally bored: I put my attention on something else—for example, played educational records and listened to them. That was one. At another period, I did free association on past tiredness and illnesses by the Freudian method, on the theory that stress of exercise would be forcing such memories closer to the surface. For me it was true.

In doing push-ups, start at the waist. That is, keep the lower portion of your body on the floor, and push up only the upper. Your ultimate goal is a hundred without stopping. Then do your push-ups, using the knees as your fulcrum. Only when you can also do a hundred from the knees without stopping, do you go to the toes—that is, raise the full body.

In leg-ups, lie on your back and raise the legs straight up. In doing the exercise, move them down about twelve inches (from the vertical), then up again. Keep doing this day after day until you can do a hundred there, too, without stopping. Then do the exercise from twelve inches off the vertical to within twelve inches of the floor. Finally, do from twelve inches off the floor to two inches.

In the third exercise, sit up. From the sit-up position, lean back about a foot, then forward. Keep at it until you can do a hundred without stopping.

This third exercise is the easiest of the three, and should be used first by women. Perhaps for a time it should be their only exercise. It is very likely that this is in fact the best of the three. It does what seems to be the key necessary thing: it stretches many of the muscles around the spine, right up into the skull.

Do these various things how long each day? There's a theory that some glands are not stimulated until after 40 minutes to an hour of exercising. So—if you can bring yourself to combine learning something from a tape, record, or radio—set yourself that 40-minute minimum, rest when you have to, but resume, and keep going.

Whatever your time, do a combination of the three, if you're a man, and number three to begin with if you're a woman.

Before doing the setting-up exercises, I did three months of jogging—40 minutes every morning. It was good for my heart and lungs and stamina, for I could eventually run up a half-mile-long hill road. But my mental energy did not improve markedly until I started push-ups and leg-ups. Later, 20 minutes of jogging a day did not, of itself, maintain me at the mental peak which I achieved with the setting-up regimen. Jogging, for me, is not enough.

The Exercise-Nap

You say you absolutely have to have that afternoon or after-dinner nap?

Try the following:

When the feeling of sleepiness hits you, take your pillow and lie down on the floor (on a rug).

Your intent—and my intent for you—is that you *are* going to have a nap. This is not a scheme to deny you that privilege.

However, when you have lain down, do a few push-ups. Or leg-ups. Or lean-backs. The easy versions.

Then, and only then, cuddle down on the pillow.

First time you awaken drowsily—again do some p.u.'s, l.u.'s or l.b.'s.

Keep doing this throughout your nap every day.

Now, understand: by this method you essentially remain in a

horizontal position for as long as you normally do when you lie down for a snooze.

Repeat this day after day—and see what presently happens. (It takes a while, so don't be impatient.)

What happens is that eventually you don't have that need for a nap.

Yogi Exercises

A psychologist friend recently demonstrated 31 Yogi exercises to me. Essentially, they were methods of tensing and relaxing (and a lot of free body swinging) all parts of the body while standing up. He said they kept him alert. He did all 31 in 20 minutes. He lost 15 pounds the first three months he did them. Information about such exercises are available from various sources, books, etc.

Some people shouldn't exercise, so why don't you visit your doctor, and get his opinion on the foregoing regimen for you.

Perhaps you prefer more authoritative advice on the type of exercise. Write for the physical fitness manuals from the U.S. Government.*

Don't want to exercise, or can't imagine yourself doing it?

Obtain Medical Advice

Then ask your doctor about a stimulant suitable for you. Whatever you take, do so the moment your energy begins to sag. Whatever you take, be sure to get a good night's sleep.

The basic idea: Don't let fatigue or a droopy mental condition slow you down from the time you get up in the morning until you go to bed.

I'm assuming that most people will not go to doctors. For you, either exercise according to your best understanding of yourself,

---

* The President's Council on Physical Fitness and Sports, Room 4049, HEW, North, 330 Independence Avenue SW, Washington, D.C. 20201.

or if you don't exercise, drink Cokes or coffee throughout the day if you are inclined to be sluggish, or take a tranquilizer if you are the overstimulated kind.

Tea is supposed to have more caffeine than coffee. In addition, it has something far greater going for it. It is one of the rare foods that contain *theophylline,* which causes a widening of the coronary artery. Anger people, who plan to use caffeine, please note. Tea is good for what anger sometimes does to hearts.

After you have made your pile by some sustained approach to staying in motion, spend some of it in making sure that you didn't damage yourself en route, and if you did, pay what's necessary for rectifying things.

At one talk I gave, there was a question from the floor about the value of 7–Up, "the uncola." My reply: "So far as I know, it's not a stimulant. Doctors often recommend it as an aid to digestion or to counteract stomach upset. I'd guess it's actually good for you, but it may not keep you awake."

FUNCTION OF AUTONOMIC NERVOUS SYSTEM

SYMPATHETIC	ORGAN	PARASYMPATHETIC
dilation	eyes	narrowing of pupils
dry eyes	lachrymal (tear) glands	sparkling eyes
dry mouth	salivary glands	mouth waters
"cold sweat"	sweat glands	dry skin
contraction	arteries	dilation
gooseflesh	skin	smooth
relaxation	bronchial muscles	stimulation
increases action	heart	depresses action
inhibits digestive action	gastro-intestinal	stimulates digestive action
stimulates adrenal secretion	endocrine glands	stimulates choline secretion.
Etc.		

We can see from the foregoing that sympathetic nervous activity is predominantly contractive, and that the parasympathetic is predominantly expansive. In a nutshell, the sympathetic system represents self-contraction—away from the world and back into the self. The parasympathetic represents the direction of expansion—out of the self and into the world.

The moment you have doubt or the feeling of failure, you are manifesting the "sympathetic" side. Do *something* immediately. Drink a Coke, and resolve (best of all) to find a way whereby you can exercise yourself into permanent good health—the parasympathetic side.

5

Fifth Quality of the Money Personality: Applying "Human Mathematics"

> In every commercial deal, the money personality always asks where the money will come from.

Now we come to the part about moneymaking that you've heard about most often. The schemes! The systems! The con games! And of course the valid plans and well-thought-out ideas:

- How Orator Woodward persisted in putting gelatin powder and flavoring into little envelopes, beginning in 1895, and made millions out of Jello.
- How Henry Rosenfeld made "class market" dresses at "mass market" prices, and became a millionaire at 35.
- How Richard Niessen Harris created the Toni Home Permanent, and at age 32 sold to Gillette for $20 million.
- How lawyer Ralph E. Schneider was motivated to start Diner's Club, the first credit card—and you know the rest of that story.

Inspirational, yes. Worth emulating, of course. To be admired—greatly.

But as a former friend of mine would say, "That ain't the way it happened, kiddies."

By this time you probably realize that a person who is a victim and/or cannot charge a profit, or lacks other key qualities, could have the best idea in the world for making money. And it will do him no good.

In fact it was not Orator Woodward who developed the idea for the first gelatin dessert. That honor belongs to Peter Cooper, who patented it in 1845—but his interest (see Personality Quality Eight) was in designing locomotives and heavy fixed machinery, so he never did anything with his gelatin dessert patent.

Cooper was very much a money maker in another field—heavy machinery. His problem with the gelatin was that he couldn't put his attention on something as apparently trivial and insubstantial as a dessert powder.

Needless to say, this is a different problem from that of the average non-money maker.

Usually, a non-money maker couldn't recognize a good money-making idea if—and I mean this literally—you paid him.

The Personal Factor in Money Making

When we look at the financially capable, we realize that not everybody is financially handicapped.

We observe a successful man using his knowledge and intelligence in a free fashion to reason his way to an optimum solution for a problem. His business grows; he becomes more successful. He asked the simple, relevant, preliminary questions, added up the facts and the people involved, and throughout remained on top of the situation.

We watch another man, stubbornly refusing to face those self-same facts, rationalize himself deeper into a problem, maintain his self-esteem at all costs as losses mount, ignore sound advice and make wrong emergency decisions without telling anyone, until finally we realize that *he* is the problem. It couldn't possibly exist in the form that it does except for what his obstinacy and irrationality contribute to it. He is constantly in a financial crisis.

Basically, of course, what is wrong is that this second man—who can be numbered in more legions than the Roman Empire could muster in its entire thousand-year existence—particularly lacks Quality Five.

First of all, such a man—most likely you, also (even though you're not that wild)—should be interested in the basic thought of where money comes from. If we could collect all the books ever written on success, and if we could place them in a giant pot and boil them down to one sentence, that sentence would be:

> Find a human need; serve that need to the best of your ability, and success is guaranteed.

So, what's the matter? Why can't you (1) either examine the world and notice an unfilled need with money potentialities? or (2) notice where you can operate with a need that has already been long observed, join the group there, and get to work?

That's all. On the surface, and *in fact,* there's nothing more to it.

Of course, we know that since you're still alive you've probably already been connected a number of times with a need-filling activity. Usually somebody else's. And of course there's got to be a cause for your not doing better, or why you're not doing this for yourself.

However, I must tell you that this section is not for you at all if you're still a victim or can't charge a profit. Don't start a restaurant and, victim-wise, reason yourself into the idea that lowering the prices will necessarily bring customers. Price is based on cost, and unless there is a cash flow well above all the costs, you're not mathematically oriented to the facts. The same applies in any other business.

My advice: If you have frequently been in such unprofitable enterprises, solve the problem first on the game level described in this section.

If you're a victim, don't even bother with money-making reasoning until you've resisted victimizers or even ordinary retail promotional methods for a year or more. Perhaps, as I did, you can pass the time recovering from your past mistakes, and meanwhile work hard at your necessity job.

Learn the Difference Between Business and Friendship

Step Five is for people like the following man:

During the Great Depression a business man on the verge of bankruptcy went to his creditors and offered them a plan whereby his business would be operated for their benefit until their debts were paid. They had not realized the seriousness of his predicament and, since their own situation was such that they could not carry him, they promptly joined together and forced him into bankruptcy. In the mid-1950's he again faced a serious financial emergency. But, remembering his earlier experience, he dared not go to his creditors and talk it over with them. Soon, under the stress of worry, he became dangerously ill. During his illness, his business went bankrupt. One of his creditors said to him later, "We were all agreed. If you had come to us in time, we could have worked it out."

One of the things that ailed this man was that he was unable to evaluate a situation *now* as being different from a situation *then*.

Most people who kept their heads above water during the Great Depression—let's look at it squarely—clutched at straws themselves. They had no room for riders. Anyone who wanted the other person's straw to support him too, wasn't using his head.

A man who observed the Great Depression from a youthful vantage point near the bottom of the stream, recalled for me how those who were actually fighting looked in action. They were non-victims to a man. Store dealers handled the cash registers themselves; employees could neither put in money nor take out change. Under pressure they robbed Peter to pay Paul, applied the grease to wheels that squeaked the loudest—and usually waited until the squeak was a scream—put on grim (i.e. strong-appearing) fronts and lay awake nights reasoning out practical solutions and not fantasy ones.

Our two-time bankrupt took none of these things into account. He tried to get a family-personal consideration, but was not a relative. Since I am looking back at him from a distance in time, it is just a surmise on my part that he lacked Quality Five. But he did fail to realize the human facts of a situation . . . which, in essence, is what Step Five is about.

With that thought, we come to the detailed account of precisely what Quality Number Five of the twelve-quality money personality is.

Learning from Games

Did you see the motion picture, *The Hustler,* a few years ago?

The lead character was played by Paul Newman, and it was all about a poolroom mathmatician who had converted arithmetic, algebra, calculus, and probably all other number systems, known and unknown, into the enormously integrated skill that goes into being a pool shark.

Mr. B., one of the three now wealthy men whom I had known as children and whose success spurred me ten years ago to undertake this study of money making (based on my knowledge of their characters), was a pool shark in his younger days.

He was great at dice, also. During his early years he made $90 a week as salesman for a tobacco company and $90 a week shooting dice. But he played his masterful pool in those scores of little towns where he had to spend his nights when he was on the road.

Today, he makes upward of $90,000 a year. In mulling over his past, I recalled this enormous pool-playing ability. I asked a psychologist about it. He told me that skill at pool and dice is considered to be indicative of a natural mathematical genius.

Mr. B. only went to Grade 10. So his formal mathematical training could be squeezed into a large thimble.

When I realized that it might take an ability to reason mathematically in order to become wealthy, I felt a great unease.

But it does. And that's Quality Five.

I hate to bring this up. Because, financially speaking, the average man cannot mathematically reason himself out of a hole in the ground.

And what about all those poor women who have always hated arithmetic?

Fortunately, the answer is simple. It's not that kind of mathematics.

Learn to Add and Subtract Human Nature

You need to be able to add two and two in the world of human behavior and make it come out four. Nearly all women can do this—in terms of money—but very few men.

The first task for any person who hasn't made his pile, and wants to, is to discover by what manner he repeatedly makes a financial idiot of himself.

I've learned that it's no use asking him to examine what he's actually doing wrong in the environment.

It may be that he can't see the forest for the trees, is too subjective, has too brief an attention span, is one of those people who spend their time doing good, is so alienated from our society that he wouldn't give it the time of day (except that he has to eat), absorbs himself in one costly hobby after another, is getting even with his wife—I could go on. The problem is how do you get a man to see what particular personal madness keeps him down in his hole?

Fortunately, he doesn't have to become sane. Some of the craziest and zaniest people on the planet have money. People who can neither read nor write—at least this was true a generation ago—have made fortunes. My observation: Money pours in golden streams to the people who have the twelve qualities that I am describing.

But if you don't have those qualities, you can lose the largest of inherited fortunes. And if you don't have quality number five—the one I'm describing—the speed at which the money goes will startle all onlookers.

A few years ago a large holding company was bought by two men who had inherited vast wealth. It seemed that one of these men had always wanted to own an insurance company, and the holding company didn't have one. Here's how he got it. He and his colleague sold a successful factory for $18 million. Then they bought an insurance company for $15 million from a man who also owned a bank. The insurance company paid an annual dividend of 1–1/2%.

During the week following their sale at the factory, the stock of the company that bought it trebled in value. When one of the two men told my friend, Mr. C., of the transaction, Mr. C. could scarcely restrain his contempt. "First of all," he said, "you sold a $40 million factory for less than half its value. And do you know what that banker probably did with your check for $15 million for that insurance company?" "No, what?" "He put it into his own bank, which pays 4% or more annual interest, while he looked around for a better investment."

The errors made by people who cannot reason such things out come under several headings, like these: They try to sell refrigerators to Eskimos in winter time, or cows to sheepherders; out of a job, they turn to writing or inventing; a city man buys a farm and hires somebody to run it.

Observe Your Money Reasoning Ability in a Game

It's only on a small screen that one can see what one does wrong in the real world, money-wise. Do you play chess? Have you ever done mathematical puzzles? Do you play cards or shoot dice? Pool? These are all mathematical games. They are the small screen where you can see what you're doing.

Until not too long ago, when I played chess I never figured beyond two or three moves ahead. It was of course the fourth move with which my opponent checkmated me. By way of comparison, let's say you can see three steps ahead in darkness, so on the strength of that you take four steps. The fourth step, of course, carries you over the edge of a cliff.

I used to be unusually good at mathematical puzzles, then I lost the ability. Recently, when I was motivated by my own theory to try a puzzle again, it took me an hour and 40 minutes before the answer flashed into my mind. Two persons, who heard the puzzle at the same time as I, had the answer in less than 30 seconds.

In analyzing what I did during that hundred minutes, I discov-

ered that I had jumped to a conclusion at the very beginning and
that I never again examined that part of the problem.

P.S. The conclusion I jumped to was false, naturally.

Taking into account the foregoing comments, I have discovered
after considerable inquiry that Section One of Rule Five consists
of two mathematically sound questions.

I mean, mathematically sound on the money reasoning level in
which two human equations added to two economic factors equal
four plus-values.

Rules of Money Reasoning (Part One)

Rule Five's first question: *"In what you're planning to do, is
there any money?"*

All over the country, over the world, people are working long
hours at tasks where—if they would stop to ask themselves this
one question—they'd break off the action right away.

In most of the things that people get involved in, even if they
were 100% successful, there is no money.

The second and last question in Rule Five, Part One, is: *"Am
I now the type of person who can make money in that area?"*

What this means is, are you capable of properly investigating
an opportunity, and are you then able to act on the basis of the
facts that you unearth?

(Do you dismiss the facts, and do it anyway, to hell with reality?
Or does the data actually have meaning for you?)

The following is a common example:

Let us suppose that you are considering a business that involves
cleanliness; your stage (a restaurant or store) has to look clean
and be clean. But you have not previously been a clean person.
Don't go into that business.

And, furthermore, don't imagine that you're going to be able
to hire somebody to keep the place clean. It doesn't work that way.

That's one part of the kind of logic that I'm telling you about.
Under no circumstances pretend to yourself that what you're
planning to do will change your character.

In finding out from a mathematical game how you reason, it

isn't so much do you win, or how quickly you win, but your step-by-step method and the emotional overtones. At what phase of your reasoning do you consider that you have taken enough factors into account?

Now, if you actually do win consistently I'd of course be inclined to deduce that Quality Number Five is not your problem. However, if your wife thinks that you're lame on mathematical reasoning in real life situations, better take a second look. She could be one of the 20 per cent of women who are losers. But a wife often can see clearly when a man is following one of those male will-o-the-wisps.

If a man does not show good sense when his wife asks him, "Is there any money here and who will pay it to you?," she'd better make up her mind that sooner or later she's going to have to go out and earn the family bread.

Rules of Money Reasoning (Part Two)

To make as sure as possible such a thing doesn't happen, I'm going to beat once more at this point. Let us suppose you're the type who gives facile, optimistic answers to the two questions of Section One of Rule Five.

You say, "It's a cinch, Joan; with a set-up like I'm getting ready, we'll have the better mousetrap that people come to look for, and I'm the guy that's got just the right kind of cheese for them."

You say, "Once I get those ads out, the orders will start to pour in with every mail delivery, and you don't have to be any kind of a special person to fill mail orders."

Et cetera.

And each time it's not true.

If such a wrongness happens *even once,* then for you the basic game analysis is mandatory.

Section Two of Rule Five: *"Discover in a game you know what's basically wrong with your money reasoning."*

And here is a thought, which I'm re-stating, emphasizing it almost at the Rule level: "It is axiomatic that, unless you have a large company structure, you can never get an employee to do well something that you cannot do yourself." This is why the heir to a small business has to learn every department, however briefly he's there. So the next time you hear the joke that the eldest son made it from office boy to vice-president in one year, laugh heartily—at yourself. You have just observed the action of an intuitively wise father-owner.

Question: How far down into the work-level does this apply?

Answer: There is no lower limit. An owner who cannot clean up his own plant will never consistently be able to get an employee to do it.

Alternate Solution: If you can afford it, hire an outside maintenance firm to do the job.

In a big company, all of the foregoing applies to the department heads.

Making Qualitative Changes

The money personality seems beyond average because he has benefited from quantitative and then qualitative changes. The successful individual is, for the easily overawed (that includes most of us when it comes to money), one of the hurdles of our existence. There he is at the height of his power. And what a height it seems to be! Young people, coming up from the uncertain teen years, and older people who somehow got sidetracked, are often deeply disturbed by the differences they see between this person and themselves. It almost seems as if no one can ever again attain such a pinnacle of understanding, easy control of vast operations, and possession of money, real estate, industry, and influence on such a scale.

Yet there was a day when this moneyed personality also was a young man, and before that a youth; a time when he also had his way to make in the world. Or, if he inherited wealth, he had the task of learning how to keep his inheritance and make it grow.

What to Do at the Bottom

To millions who are at the very bottom of the economy, who can't even hold a steady job, I suggest this: Take a look at what you do when you're not working.

Do you waste time? For example, do you bum away your unemployment insurance time? If so, you've got a lot of alienation in you against our society.

Do you daydream? That is, decide that maybe now is when you should start commercializing a talent which you've always felt you had for art painting, composing music, story writing, or inventing? It's the *wrong* time. The proof of a genuine interest in an artistic endeavor, or in the merit of an invention, is the energy with which you pursue the matter in your spare time *when you have a job*. Do you somehow never get around to it? That usually tells the real story. Forget it.

When you're at the bottom is also probably not the time for you to become an activist. You're at the necessity level of life. You need a job, and you should take the best offer you can get and hold onto it uncomplainingly. If there is to be a complaint against what your boss is paying you, it should be as part of a union drive with other employees. If you are a new employee, it's not up to you to spark the rebellion or to be one of the hotheads.

If there's no chance of a raise, use your reason and get some training—if that is what you lack. And as soon as possible look for another job that pays more.

I repeat: At this stage you do not handle a job situation in a way that will endanger your necessity income. Your task is to stabilize yourself on a springboard so you can make your second move.

There are two ways to make Move Two.

Decide Which Type You Are

One of them is to work toward being a valuable employee; the other is to go into business for yourself.

The reasoning here: If you are for our society as it is, essentially, then you should not hesitate to acquire the training that will make you a more valuable, and valued, employee in some good company.

If, on the other hand, you are against our society—i.e., are an alienated person, a non-conformist in your thinking—essentially you should mark time while you are working for someone else, keep your non-conformism to yourself, and as soon as you reason it out correctly, go into business.

In this latter instance, during this period of working while you gather your energies for the big jump into your own business, you must prove that you are more than an average non-victim and must acquire a very firmly held reason for charging a profit.

There Is a Method by Which You, Too, Can Save

The proof that you are a genuine non-victim is that during this period no matter what pleasures you have to deny yourself or how much you may look like a cheapskate, you must save approximately 25% of your income. Believe it or not, this is what the naturals are doing and have always done. This is how they got their start.

One of many books I read on money-making was an odd treasure called *The Richest Man in Babylon.* Among the gems in this book was "Seven Cures for a Lean Purse." However, the first prescribed cure was, "Save ten percent of what you make." The idea is good. The percentage is inadequate. It would take years at that rate to acquire a nest egg. So—I repeat earnestly—it's got to be more than double that. But actually such a saving can be achieved in various ways, as for example through the second "cure."

The second cure prescribed was, "When you have saved some money, invest it wisely." Combine the two thoughts, is my suggestion. Save enough for a down payment on some worthwhile investment, and then make your payments the equivalent of 22% or 23% of your income.

I'll pick up that suggestion again in my discussion of Qualities Eight and Twelve, and you'll see that it has a two-edged value.

Realizing the potentiality of one's assets requires all the mathematical reasoning one can muster, and that is as true of holding onto a fortune already made as of making one.

Your Response in a Game Is Your Key to Business Reasoning

Notice that I am not telling you or anyone *what* your business-wise reasoning should be. If you have wormed or inherited your way up to some high echelon of our economic aristocracy you will know that management decision-making always relates to a specific business. There are basic administration principles, true, but in most instances the ramifications of any big business require from the executive years of experience and the ability to analyze extremely detailed happenings.

But what I *am* saying is that if you play chess, or cards, or do mind twisters, you can observe the errors in your decision-making reasoning because what you do on this tiny level you will repeat on the larger scene.

Is your key response to the puzzle *impatience?* Observe the same emotion on the business level. Do you not take the time to understand the problem? You're doomed. Do you play the game casually? Take an uncasual look at the relaxed pose with which you conduct your business. Do you lose in the game? How? Notice the details of that one for absolute certain.

The foregoing applies to a presently successful man who has some reason to be concerned about the future. And of course it applies to all persons who are not presently being successful.

Now, if you're the boss, and you play bridge or poker with your top executives, be careful how you evaluate their game skill. You may be a super-egotist, or even a rival of God in your own secret heart. Top executives soon find out such personality madness in the Chief and sadly react to it—for example—by losing to you consistently, or enough.

Besides, an employee doesn't necessarily have to be able to reason soundly on his own behalf. If he were that smart, you might be working for him.

At this point I hope all you future money-makers are carrying several cards, each with a rule written on it——these rules which, when frequently glanced at, will become a part of your automatic thinking and acting.

If you are a person of normal ambition and drive, and are

presently in motion (doing things, earning money, willing, and not resisting, not alienated) then these rules *by themselves* are probably sufficient guides for you at the present time.

However, if you have suffered setbacks, if you can't seem to get interested, or interest is faltering; if things don't mean as much as they used to, if there's been a let-up in the old go, or you can't seem to get started, etc., then you'd better make a sharp study of the remaining qualities.

A Winner at Games and Business

I recently came across a vivid picture of what a card player's method reveals about him.

In his autobiographical book, *The Education of a Broadcaster,* NBC Vice-President Harry Bannister describes how he plays gin rummy. His description gives a perfect example in miniature of the kind of reasoning he undoubtedly did in the larger game of being a top NBC executive:

> Regardless of stakes, I always play gin the same way, coldly, impersonally and totally . . . memorizing each card as it falls. Before I make any discard, I rapidly calculate the chance of its being used in my opponent's hand, and I always make the discard with the lowest percentage possibility of being picked up. All this sounds like hard work, but I have always enjoyed problems in mental arithmetic. . . . (Such) mathematical play, against normal opposition, is hard to beat. . . . If we play long enough, I nail my opponent in the end. . . . I've never played "customer" gin with anyone, and never will . . . so I usually end up a winner.

And with a goodly supply of cash to show for his long and interesting life, as well.

P.S. Don't invest in a non-friend's business, invention, or idea —unless the amount is small, you recognize the High Risk, and you will not be hurt financially if you lose every penny. Or, unless you are *supremely* experienced in the matter involved.

P.P.S. There are some emergency, or business, situations in our economy for which a person cannot obtain needed funds from a bank or loan company. He can only borrow it from relatives or friends. If you are a close relative (or friend), then you are a potential source of money for him at such a time. How much should you loan him? Unless you are willing to make him a gift, loan him only what he can pay back on the basis of his *present* possession of the twelve qualities that I have described.

6

Sixth Quality of the Money Personality: Developing Realistic Competitiveness

The money personality competes for real rewards, not for illusions.

At the present time, the United States' share of the world's work is done by people who receive varying rates of pay for what they do. In other countries, including the Communist, the pay scale is lower; but there also it varies.

Everywhere, the more pay you get the more sumptuously you can live. Hence, most people early in life are motivated to compete for, and seek out, higher pay positions.

Some succeed. Most fail.

Why do people fail?

First of all, of course, we have in growing numbers the person who won't play the game of what his type calls the establishment. He refuses to recognize the current standards of success, or he has an automatic rebellious response to any kind of authority.

"I didn't ask to be born, so I don't feel bound by the rules of this world," some of these people will tell you.

Most of us look around at the blue skies, the grandeur of the mountains, the silent, beautiful rivers—yes, even though polluted —and the numberless horizons of earth, and we are relieved that we are indeed among those who were born, and what is more, born human.

Still, as we come up from the mists of childhood, we are made aware that all is not cake and ice cream. There are chores to be done, and, presently, a living to make by rules that have been in existence for a long time. We anxiously scan our environs, and ask: "What are the rules of this game? And what's the score?"

At first sight the score seems to be fiercely against us. Everywhere we turn are all those older people who got here first. And they own everything. There's not an acre, not a piece of timber, not a building nor an item of equipment that hasn't got someone else's name on it, with a sign up and a finger pointing at you. The sign says, in effect: "Keep out! Do not touch. This is private (or government) property."

Competition Can Mean Many Things

Some parents are wise enough to inform their offspring that an education is the key to the future competition they will run into.

Notice the word "competition." It doesn't really mean what it seems to.

Fortunately, in many enlightened countries, the initial steps of education are compulsory. You really have to work hard at refusing to play by the rules, to avoid learning to spell and do figures.

I've met a few young fellows recently who worked so hard at resisting that they still write like little children, their bodies all tightened up as they slowly make the configurations of written English, misspelling even simple words.

For them, things don't look good. Jail? Welfare? Manual labor?

A combination, I would guess—unless they start thinking hard. I recommend the armed forces with their advanced technical training for these young adults, with the intention finally of somehow going into business for themselves. At the turn of the century, and since, many an illiterate was successful in his own business.

Whichever he chooses, he and others will be competing (if that's the right word) for the world's goods.

Competing to Win

Pause, now, while we consider what we mean by competition.

In competing, some portion of your brainwashing is more important than other portions in slowing you down, or diverting you from what you should be doing.

If you believe in regular hours—that's an example.

The concept of regular hours implies rules, regulations; everyone waiting at the same starting line for someone to fire the gun. When it is fired, we all leap forward and, with the rules continuing to guide our conduct, we lope along in our little lane taking care not to encroach on anyone else's. Soon, the gun is fired again; and it's coffee break time. Then, later, lunch, and finally quitting time. Whereupon we all go home.

Like hell we do!

I have to tell you that there were some early birds out. They left the starting line at dawn, or before, and didn't call it quits until the night was black and the eyes were bleary, and the need for sleep could no longer be denied.

That manufacturer I mentioned in the Victim-Non-Victim section—his wife told me that when he was developing his products, she would be aware of him in the adjoining twin bed, turning, tossing.

Awakening at 3 A.M., she would fine him gone—to the little shop, in the rear of which he did his developmental work. Daytimes in those days he was an aircraft engineer employed by one of the big companies.

> "Ye've got to get oop prrretty airly in the mairnin' t' get ahaid o' Sandy MacPherson."

If that isn't an old Scotch saying, it should be.

What it tells you is that the principal rule governing competition is willingness to be where it counts; as General Forrest said in the American Civil War, get there "fustest with the mostest."

What's fair? It's amazing the ideas that people have on this subject that defeat them before they ever get started.

An historical example: In Hannibal's day, the Roman armies fought during the daytime and slept at night. Daytime seems like the proper time for a battle, you'll agree. But on the mornings of major engagements Hannibal's armies were on the move by 3 A.M. Roman soldiers awakened in time to die without even being able to grab their weapons. Was that fair?

Time came when a Roman general noticed Hannibal's little 3 A.M. pattern. On the day that the great Carthaginian finally went down to disaster, the Roman armies were up at 2 A.M., and about the time Hannibal's forces started to move, the Roman legions were upon them.

In pitch darkness!

Unfair, uncomfortable, anxiety-producing, nation-destroying? Yes. The result: It was the end forever of Carthage as an imperial competitor in the Mediterranean. Rome went on from that battle to become the leading power of the ancient world for hundreds of years.

If you read what I have just described to mean that to win you must be unfair, then you are missing the point.

It is *you* who are caught up in the fairness-unfairness dichotomy.

Many Levels of Competition

What I'm telling you is that neither fairness nor unfairness is a factor in successful "competition."

The boss needs somebody in a key position who will be loyal to him. Breaking that down, we deduce that he wants someone who accepts the employer-employee relations; agrees, in short, that there is such a thing as a boss, and such a status as hired help.

So Wes, who fits that description, is promoted. Both Wes and his wife feel that his new job proves that he is being a winner in the world of competition. But—

The boss selected Wes because he saw in him a person who would *not* be in competition with him (the boss).

Am I saying that Wes should be disloyal to his boss, once he gets the job?

Not at all.

Then what?—

Well, friend, it's all right to be an employee, but it's not all right to think like one. There's no question that certain big jobs in this world can be done only within the frame of vast companies or the even vaster operation of a government, but that's a reality which you observe rationally—and then you start to figure how you in your present status can get in on the deal.

First thing to notice: Those who are hired as employees have a fixed rate of pay. If that's the best you can do to start with, that's what you do. But remember, it takes an act of Congress to raise your wages when you operate in that category. In such situations, the raise, when voted, is usually a small percentage for everyone. It comes out to perhaps $5 a week across the board.

Why don't you leave that level of operation to the people who haven't read this book?

The big money goes to the contractors, and the slightly less (but big enough) money to the sub-contractors. You can also be a sub-sub-contractor on one item to a sub-contractor's part of the job.

So long as you have to work for someone, be loyal, faithful, industrious, pay your bills, and be responsible.

But don't get hung up in a dead-end job for the rest of your life. In due course, after you have promoted your own welfare in your spare time, obtain an honorable discharge from your employer and go about the business of making money for yourself.

When should you make such a move?

Not until your spare time is bringing in a substantial sum on a regular basis. Use your God-given reason with a big dose of Quality Five to determine the exact time.

Remember, you are competing for money, not a job, not an ego-boost, not the satisfaction of beating out someone else for a $10-a-week raise (though you should do that also an an intermediate act).

When you finally have money, ego satisfaction and a sense of power will come automatically.

So add to the cards you carry around with you (and all of which you look over several times a day), one that has the following simple statement written on it:

I compete for money.

There's more to observe about competition.
(Read on, quickly!)

Refusing Labels That Limit You

The money personality does not label himself by the type of job he does.

People soon discover that if they apply for a position outside of the narrow range of their previous experience or education, their application is ordinarily tossed aside.

If you can't do bookkeeping, don't ask for a bookkeeper's job.

I hasten to point out that I recognize that you know as well as I that what I have just said is obvious in terms of the employer's attitude.

Engineers are hired for their engineering training, architects for architecture, and order clerks for related work.

Question: How can you get richer than what is provided by the money paid for the particular task that you're trained to do? "I," you say, "have training as a file clerk. What do *I* do?"

Answer: You adopt an attitude, to start.

The same attitude should be adopted by a person with a degree in engineering or by anyone who possesses *any* training, no matter how advanced.

The point is: Don't label yourself. J. Paul Getty, in his interesting book *The Golden Age,* rejects the idea that human beings are limited. I reject it, also. There is no such human being as a bookkeeper or an engineer. If you have a training of some kind, and somebody—some employer or personnel director—tries to narrow you in on that tiny channel, maybe at that moment you have to let him do so. He doesn't know any better, poor limited creature.

But in your secret mind, do not accept such a designation. If you say to me, " But I *am* an engineer,"—boy, oh boy, are you missing the thought! The thought is that your engineering training is one of your credits. Use it like a king or an ace in a game of cards, or like the queen in chess. But don't ever let it be the *only* piece in your mind.

First Unlabeling Therapy: Stop Labeling Yourself

On the white card for Quality Six, write:

I herewith cease labeling myself as _____ [*your job*].

Training is a systematic thought or awareness about some process level in nature or society. Congratulations on having acquired that training. But if, on the day you got your sheepskin testifying to that training, and *labeling you* accordingly, you did an ego-superiority thing—that's it. Your mind probably blew right there. You're hung up on that label, and you've got the job of climbing from the pigeonhole you fell into.

An even worse condition, of course, is that of the person who has no special high level training. Most such persons eventually acquire job experience but the process is very labeling, also, and usually has associated with it an ego-reducing pattern. The combination creates an even deeper pigeonhole. When you peer down into the darkness, there at the bottom sits the individual, and he looks up at you and in effect says, "This is what I am. This is where I belong."

Second Unlabeling Therapy: Refuse to Label Others

There is another side to our tendency to label.

We spend our early years in a world of people who have achieved super-images: presidents of companies and rulers of nations, sports champions and war heroes, owners of property and possessors of special knowledge—men and women who had already made it, or who had been born into great positions before we even learned how to spell.

They were labeled for us by the world. Unnoticing, we picked up the labels and made them our own. Thereafter we felt *less*. For us, after we accepted those labels, there were people in faraway places who seemed larger than human.

We have to rid ourselves of such labels without—and hear this!—disparaging their achievements.

You've all heard the person who says of a well-known figure: "Aw, he's not so much."

He's trying by disparagement to throw off the effect of having been overwhelmed by a label in his early years. His real problem: He accepted the label. Now, it weighs on him.

The whole of history swarms with brave and brilliant and beautiful and delightful and creative human beings. Don't lift yourself by putting them down. It's a negative approach.

Just un-label yourself.

How?

Write the following on the other side of the "label" card:

> I will no longer label _____ or any other famous or authoritative person by what he has done or by the position he holds or has held.

In the blank space write in pencil the name of some person of whom you have stood in awe. Keep the name there for a while, then erase it and write in (again in pencil) some other awesome name. By this method you will soon dispose of your false inner picture of people who are actually just as human as you—as you will discover once you get to know them.

The difference is that in their field of achievement they learned to act within the frame of one or more systematic trainings. In your field you must learn to do the same, so that eventually you never react with just an opinion or a feeling. In that area of knowledge you respond only with your systematic thought.

(Among other things, most of these famous people undoubtedly had naturally many of the twelve qualities I am describing in this book.)

The Difference Between a Label and an Assignment

Now—one more thought here which, at first look, may seem contradictory.

Top management people that I have talked to feel that it is a good thing for a man to identify himself closely with his profession or job or company.

Yes, you read that correctly.

They want you to feel: "I am a technician in the electronics division." . . ."I am an engineer." . . . "I am a _____ [*any kind of specialist*]." . . . The belief here is that it is good for you to have such an association with your work.

There is a truth here. People feel better, more stable, when they are identified with anything good. The moment the boss says to you, "Archie, from this moment you will be in charge of this desk, and answering this phone," he points a direction for you, and gives you a guideline and—more important—a feeling of belonging. Unless you quit the firm, that's the location where you will be located in future, doing what is required of the person who occupies that key spot.

Looks like labeling, doesn't it?

It isn't. It's an assignment.

You must learn to distinguish between the two. I assure you the human mind is capable of operating within the frame of such refined considerations.

Do *not* identify yourself with your assignments except in a kind of way. To make money for you, and not just for top management, you must progressively seek, or give yourself, assignments that will lead you to greater affluence. Be sure, on each successive assignment, that you carry it out exactly as if you are identified with it. But the truth is your identity is something greater, something much more flexible and capable of growth.

Here's another way to move off a label:

Start taking adult-level evening courses once a week in practical, down-to-earth technologies: bookbinding, real estate, interior decorating, touch typing, camera operation and home film development, elementary electronics (learn to fix your own TV set), etc.

To enter such a course you must before a new semester starts obtain a pamphlet from your local high school or college. This pamphlet lists adult education evening courses available. Some courses are quickly filled up, so on registration night have an alternative or two in mind.

Once signed up, go once a week.

It can't be totally out of the question, particularly if you start taking your after-work nap on the floor, as described elsewhere.

Once you have a basic training in something interesting, you can begin earning extra money at home in your spare time.

That's how my millionaire manufacturer (now retired—in his forties) started. He was an aircraft engineer daytimes, and at night he repaired TV sets. Soon he opened his own repair shop—and still had his job. From there to inventing and manufacturing was not quite as big a step.

He is now one of the gnomes of Zurich—meaning he has his money in a numbered account in Switzerland, and loans his money on short terms to banks at 12% interest. Really.

7

Seventh Quality of the Money Personality: Acquiring a Common Touch

Even the most arrogant money personality knows that he has to have some friends and some wellwishers.

A number of people who considered following the Dale Carnegie system, as outlined in his huge bestseller *How to Win Friends and Influence People,* told me that they were offended by the apparent requirement in the theory of flattering individuals you wanted to influence. It seemed to them that pretending to like people you didn't like, and toadying to a bunch of arrogant "bigshots" was more hypocrisy than they were capable of.

What is wrong with this critical attitude, and right with Dale Carnegie's approach (except—and I say this modestly—that he didn't understand it, and I do), is what I am now about to explain.

The intense interest of Napoleon in every detail of a thousand crafts, arts, and industries, made him a walking encyclopedia—so his biographers have revealed. When studying the sheep industry of France, Napoleon invited experts from all branches of the industry, including sheepherders, to visit him in his beautiful palace. Julius Caesar, the most famous Roman of all time, during his campaigns in Gaul and Britain, ate with his men in camp, lived their rough life, went everywhere with them—and simultaneously kept up with the intricacies of the political situation in the faraway capital of the world of that day.

Interest in, and reasoning about, details in the way Napoleon and Caesar did has to do with Quality Five: the mathematics of the human equation. Pretty important, often decisive; and here seen—in these men—at some peak of intensity.

Observers were not wrong to notice these qualities in the great men I have described so briefly. But, in stressing that aspect, they missed something else.

Going along with this quality was another ability of equal if not greater importance. I can't quite believe that I am describing it for the first time, but certainly Napoleon's biographers show no sign of having spotted it.

Napoleon had what I shall tentatively call a high social I.Q. What does that mean?

The private secretary of a famous playwright said to me at a party a few years ago, "My boss thinks all women are beautiful, and he *means* it—imagine!" she said in a scathing tone.

Will Rogers long ago spoke a phrase which has been reported tolerantly ever since: "I never met a man I didn't like," said Will.

That statement seems absolutely incredible to discriminating onlookers. What, *never?*

I asked various people what they thought about the remark. Most didn't take it seriously. It was an obviously phony stance, they felt, typical of many public figures maintaining their image for the easily duped.

That may be true, but I can tell you right now that what I have been describing with those two examples is the key to high social I.Q. So, basically, it's not phony.

Nature of a High Social I.Q.

Let's go back now, and look at what Napoleon *did.*

Historians and biographers noticed his interest in things, in science, in details—as I have described.

I want you to ignore that. That is another characteristic (Quality Five). In this instance, it drew the attention of the observers away from the other factor.

That factor is: Napoleon could stand having large numbers of "lower class" people around him; have them, so to speak, in his house and at his table.

I have to tell you that there are haughty people who cannot tolerate having the "lower classes" near them without being offended. The "upper classes"—kings, noblemen—of Napoleon's time and earlier, seeing a sheepherder inside a palace, would tend to react with: "Who let this dog in here?"

Whichever way you are, it shows in the long run. You can't help it.

Everywhere in the world (well, almost everywhere) descendants of such snooty types have lost their power—which their ancestors maintained by force and violence; or, if they have not yet been deprived of their hereditary positions, they are in the process of being so divested.

At this point, I'd better pause for the benefit of certain appalled, skeptical, or resisting readers. If right now you are hastily scanning over your rich acquaintances, noting how many of them are aloof and unapproachable and manifesting other behaviors contrary to what I have just said—reserve your judgment, please.

These days, it is possible to make and keep money while operating from a hidden location. When you possess certain of the twelve qualities, you don't in every situation need all of them.

Besides, unless you are a really excellent non-victim, once you actually have money the pressure from would-be borrowers can become positively unbearable. The kind of non-victimism that stood you in sufficient stead on your way up, isn't enough of a barrier when everyone finally knows you've got the stuff in large quantities. Eager sharers sense your weakness, and press their beggary. It can be very embarrassing. People avoid this by withdrawing behind the barrier of exclusiveness.

I suggest you become a better non-victim. This requires a thought. *An example:* Say that you give to causes and not to individuals. *Another:* Just shake your head, and smile enigmatically. *Another:* Tell them to write to your secretary. When the begging letter arrives, have her then write back and say that Mr. (you) gives only to causes.

Of course, you *can* be a rich S.O.B., and survive. In fact, many people *after* they get rich begin to feel free to show certain obnoxious attitudes and feelings which they took great care to suppress on the way up.

Whenever a person (on the way up) has to interrelate with people, he has to have some of the quality I am now describing. Is he a storekeeper? If he is, he comes forward with a genial smile. Or else—hear this!—he remains out of sight in his office in the back of the shop, while an employee does the honors. Needless to say, this employee is the type who drives not customers away.

She has, and people like her have, a kind of basic confidence (a high social I.Q.).

How do you get to be that confident?

Brace yourself for the incredibly simple truth.

Key to Confidence

Confidence consists of the ability to say hello, and congratulations, and to clearly enunciate your name, and to be able to hear one word when it is spoken—*the other person's name.*

Or, if you do not hear that word the first time, to have the courage to ask that it be repeated.

You say, "No, no, confidence is a feeling that you get from being somebody."

I say no, confidence is what I have just said.

Most people can *feel* a congratulatory emotion toward another person in only about four situations during that person's life: when the person graduates, gets married, is promoted, has a child. That's it. With some individuals, even this is perfunctory. And they themselves expect to be congratulated *only* during such milestone moments, but often they don't feel they've earned it even then.

Making Yourself Popular

Remember the people I mentioned at the beginning of this chapter, who felt that what Dale Carnegie wanted them to do was toady or pretend—and they couldn't be that phony. They're the ones who cannot say, or feel, congratulations for someone else, except in some terribly limited way.

If you are like this, then you're going to have to make an effort to change that narrow world you live in.

Before I tell you the method of change, let me take up a couple of the objections that you may have.

What appalls many people in such a concept is a false conclusion which they draw from it. One woman said to me, "If I really believed what you say, then I'd have to marry in an indiscriminate fashion—any bum—and have that kind of person around my house all the time."

This is really misreading the thought.

In a way Napoleon did that when he married Josephine. But presently a rational thought percolated, and he married for reasons of national security an Austrian princess.

The majority of the men and women of the United States still only marry once in a lifetime, and, like everyone else, they have only 24 hours a day to work, eat, enjoy, associate, and sleep.

Such a forever marriage should be with someone of similar tastes and similar backgrounds. When Miss Accustomed-to-Millions settles with her "bum" husband in a one-room apartment, she doesn't have to learn to dislike him in order to have the rational realization that such a life is not for her.

When Miss Middle Class marries Bohemian Artist, and comes home from work one day (she's supporting him) to find him in bed with the blonde from next door, she doesn't have to have a feeling of hatred to realize that her marriage is a mismatch for her. Thereafter, she can be friendly with artists, but when they broach a more intimate relation, she can smile and say, "Sorry, it's not my kind of existence—but go ahead and live it for youself, if you can find enough blondes to share it with you."

Preferably, she should have had enough Quality Five—sound

reasoning about "human mathematics"—to avoid an unsuitable marriage in the first place. But at twenty we are seldom as wise as at twenty-two.

As for whom you invite to your home—how big is the place, what kind of people do you like to talk to, how much time do you have for other people? Selection becomes absolutely imperative.

Your Antagonisms Tell You About You

I have had the ironic experience of witnessing both sides of the antagonistic madness that so many people manifest. At a party, a man in an adjoining chair said to me, "An affair like this is hard on me. Look at all those rats over there"—he indicated a half-dozen men who were chatting in a far corner, then went on—"laughing and joking as if they've actually got human feelings."

A little later, I happened to be talking to one of the "rats." Suddenly, he broke off, grabbed my arm, and said, "Let's get out of here, and go down the street, and have a cup of coffee. This place is really loaded with creeps tonight."

"For example," I said, "who? Creeps, I mean."

Whereupon, he pointed at a group of people which included the first man who had spoken to me.

So you see, if you have the idea that you are groveling to the creeps when you say "hello" and "congratulations" to people, this is *you* showing *your* hang-ups. It is you adding your darkness to the universe. You and all those other restricted types are creating the very world which you—by blaming and finding fault—presume to despise.

Your solution: Get another of those little white cards. Write on it: "Hello, all you good people!" and "Congratulations, everybody!"

You might even keep two lengthening lists. One might detail whom you said hello to during the course of the day, and how warm each greeting was. The second should list new qualities you have noticed in others for which you can say congratulations.

There's more to this decisive subject.

The Really Great Men of History Have Had a Common Touch.

Is what I have been saying about Quality Seven related to positive thinking?

(I think we'd better clear that up.)

Millions of people have spent half a lifetime consciously thinking positively. Whenever they have a negative thought—and become aware of it—they hastily utter something that a positive-think system has taught them.

Years ago, I noticed a woman silently moving her lips. She had closed her eyes to do so. She had just blasted a mutual acquaintance with an exceptionally nasty remark. When I saw her lips obviously forming unspoken words, I said, "Why don't you say it aloud?"

She hesitated. Then she opened her eyes, and said, "I just realized I was being negative. So I said a love poem to myself."

I said, "How long have you been doing positive thinking?"

About eight years, it turned out. That's a long time, and at first sight hers would seem to be a failure record: to have so much venom left in her—because she really had made a dark, dark negative remark about our friend. But the truth is, positive thinking is better than the continuous poison some persons spit forth. Better to try to cancel a negation than to leave it accumulated somewhere inside you.

My observation is that positive thinking has a valuable place in any individual's personality maintenance program. But it's too general.

Another example: A man reported a boy coming to his door with doughnuts to sell. The boy's opening words were: "You wouldn't want to buy a dozen of these doughnuts?" And of course —this man said—when the sales pitch was worded like that, he didn't.

Nonetheless, being of a kindly disposition, he invited the boy into his house, drilled him in a more positive approach to selling, and when the boy had the "right" positive attitude, bought his doughnuts and sent him on his way. Presumably, the boy would now become a more successful salesman for all time.

Anything wrong with this? No, not really.

Basic Confidence Is the Best "Line"

Except—a good salesman *is*. The kind of pitch he makes can be negative *or* positive. But throughout he continues to *be*.

He has confidence.

Which means that he has his own free way of saying hello. He can speak his own name without any problem of communication. And he can ask for, and hear, the other person's name. Now if the other individual does have difficulty in giving his name, and mumbles it, our Mr. High Social I.Q. Confidence can ask him to repeat it, and can repeat it after him, and somehow at the same time put over the givingness of personal warmth implicit in the meaning of congratulations, as I am presenting it in this book.

No doubt all these ideas are related: positive thinking, the positive approach, congratulations, and a reaching way of saying, "Hello, there!"

What I'm recommending here you can do *in toto* this very day. It's simple. It can be practiced by anyone, and it has underlying it a basic thought about a possible goal of the human race.

What do people really want?

They want to be creative and have all barriers down between them and other individuals.

Does that sound farfetched? *All* barriers down? Could that be true? In a way, of course, no. But basically, yes.

It might well be that altruistic human relations are the finest "good business" for a country or for a person.

I make a challenge. If you should ever open a store, or if you already have a shop of some kind, do the following:

If you are a woman, when a customer comes in, whether it's a man or a woman, flutter forward. Introduce yourself by name. Keep going toward the person. Put your arms lightly around him, your hands on his shoulders—lightly. Lean forward, and if it's a woman, kiss her on the cheeks, and if it's a man, kiss him on his lips. Then step back and say, "The way you looked when you came in was so impressive! What's your name?"

If you are a man in business, kiss the woman on the cheek, and shake hands warmly with the man.

In no case assume any kind of sexual implication or convey even the slightest sense of carnal interest.

There are variations you can do on that perfect approach. The variations are all steps down to a lower level of initial greeting—like introducing yourself by name and taking your customer's arm when he expresses his purpose in coming into the store.

When you have heard the person's name, write it down. In your diary that night, try to write it from memory. If you can't remember, find the card on which you wrote it, and copy it.

Next time this customer enters your store, at the moment when you flutter forward, address him (her) by name and at a convenient moment repeat your own as a reminder.

If you can consistently do what I have just outlined, and do it to some extent, your little shop will blossom into an oasis and you will become as rich as your bookkeeper permits.

I mention the bookkeeper because all kinds of nice young women who open up little shops have one bad habit. They think all the money that comes in is profit. Or they get the feeling that after a splurge of their own—a trip, a new car, a better apartment—they shouldn't be expected to face all those silly bills.

If you are a customer (and you read this book), in entering a store you might give your name, and learn the dealer's name, and the next time you go in, address him (her) by name. This could lead to some interesting bargains after a while.

And both of you, always remember:

   —I never met a man I didn't like. *(Will Rogers)*
   —My playwright employer thinks all women are beautiful
   —and he really means it!

People say caustically, "Did Will Rogers ever meet the guy down the street who . . . ?" (You fill in the rest of the sentence, because on every block there lives a person who is impelled by early brainwashing to "go against" in a way that can be very disturbing.)

Or they ask, "And did your boss happen to meet Mrs. Stokes, who was the plainest girl that ever lived in our town? Today at 42 that plainness has matured into ugliness."

Yes, Will Rogers knew that man on your block. Or somebody like him.

And yes, the author of that great play has seen several Mrs. Stokes's, and thinks they're all delightful.

Now, I'm telling you—you don't have to look for reasons why it's all right for them to be the way they are. When you've said hello often enough, and found more things to congratulate people for, reasons will begin to fly through some feeling level of your being.

And in case you didn't notice, kissing is the ultimate way of saying hello in a nice way.

Gradational scale on hello could be something like:

THE "HELLO" SCALE

"Hello." (Muttered, barely audible, suppressed.)
"Hello." (Shyly.)
"Hello." (Clear enough, but minimum.)
"Hello, there." (This is getting on the positive side.)
"Hi."
"Hello!" (With pleasure.)
"Hello." (Grabbing the other person's hand.)
"Hello." (Variations on touching or kissing—"going toward.")

Interesting, isn't it, that Osmanlis the Turk had the instinct to hold a cup of hot liquid to a "lowly" soldier's lips, and the patience to stand on the chow line filling the plates of his rough, hardy men with food? And let's not forget Julius Caesar who ate with *his* men.

I speculate that for the phenomenon to be visible here and there throughout history there has to be a center in the brain itself, which has been largely suppressed in most of us by early brain-washing.

And notice the communes which the young people are crowding into across the land. Here we have the desire to live together, the need to be with others.

The action of love?

Fortunately, we don't have to decide now about such controversial matters.

Learn to say "hello" and "congratulations," and you will soon have an experiential definition of your very own.

8

Eighth Quality of the Money Personality: Making Things Real and Important

By some kind of mental energy the money personality can create things that never existed before.

What's real—in terms of money making?

Answer: To him that hath shall be given. *Paraphrase:* To him that can make dreams real. *Paraphrase:* To him that has the Personality Quality Number Eight that I am about to describe, shall be given.

No one else!

You may say, "What about people who inherit?"

I've actually already answered that, but here it is again: If they don't have a proper proportion of the twelve qualities, they'll lose the money.

Many provident people, now dead, who had the twelve qualities, set up trusts for a wife and children whom they considered incapable on their own of holding onto the accumulated property, stock, and money they were inheriting.

Wise parents, these—but only up to a point. An intermediate non-money person can be protected by such a trust fund. The sad sack non-money person cannot.

You may be sure that each month when the income of these

numerous trusts comes in, as many things happen as there are people who can't hold on to money, and there is no law to protect them from their own "folly"—the absence of the twelve qualities.

Could they put the income in hock, in advance? Tens of thousands of trust income recipients have sold their trust income and never see a penny of it.

Has a human leech, or group of leeches—see Quality Twelve—found them? Then the leech is sucking the trust income dry while the actual recipient is helpless to resist.

At least, you may say enviously, such a person, however much he is being abused or has abused his inheritance, at least had some money to begin with. He has no one to blame but himself if he loses it. I—you say—never had any money to start me off.

This is true.

Some People Can Make Money but Cannot Keep It

But the truth is that thousands of people can receive money as a result of their work, but they cannot hold onto it any better than the trust inheritors whom I have just described.

The rule that I gave at the beginning of this section applies. If they can make money at all, they have some portion of Personality Quality Number Eight in their makeup.

But having made the money they can't keep it. How come?

They continue making it. But the money continues to slip through their fingers until one day they can't make money any more. How explain that?

First of all, losing the money is not an aspect of Quality Eight. That's either Number One (victim) or Number Twelve.

The explanation for why they can make money for a long time—never mind where it goes—and then one day they can't make it any more, is, alas, all too simple: they had Quality Number Eight, and then they lost it.

Of such a person it can be said that he didn't know that he had Quality Eight when he he had it. Not knowing what it was, he didn't notice when he was losing it. When it was gone, he didn't know what it was he had lost.

Sometimes a person who could both make money and hold onto it reaches an age or a state where his family take him into court and petition that a guardian be appointed for his estate and for him. When this is actually a truth, that is, when somehow the money is slipping away from him in a dramatically rapid fashion, we are witnessing the same phenomenon. Here is someone who originally had the dozen qualities, including particularly Eight, and now he has just as accidentally lost them.

Such a person who has now been declared in effect weakminded is probably no more mentally incompetent than are ordinary have-nots. But as the millions of dollars are victimized away from him, and he rationalizes his losses, he surely looks like somebody whose marbles are dropping out fast.

If you have no money, remember this is how incompetent you are *all the time.* And the fact is if a court could only be persuaded to supervise your money-making and money-retaining career, no-money-you would start to accumulate an estate almost right away.

Since this will not happen, let me repeat: money will flow to a person with a strong dose of Quality Eight. Moreover—only to the extent that you have Quality Eight, however tiny the portion, can you keep even the worst job in the world.

If you don't have some Quality Eight, *you cannot make any money* PERIOD!

By this time you will certainly be wondering what this remarkable personality ingredient can possibly be. Well—Quality Eight is the ability to make a thought real.

How the blankety-blank, you ask, do you do that?

Thereby hangs a tale, or two, or three.

Finding Meaningful Interest in Your Work

The money personality has a special, intense, meaningful interest in his work.

For centuries we've had the idea that women solve their problems by emotion and men solve theirs by gathering information and then thinking logically. Meaning, men deduce and induce and women feel; and when either has finally come to a conclusion, or is in action, on the basis thereof, a deep stubbornness sets in, and they can do or think or feel no other.

People didn't look closely enough into this phenomenon. It has a broader spectrum. There's a deeper meaning. And it can change.

A person actually solves his problems according to what's real for him. This is his philosophy, chiseled out of the rock of his experience. It's his world-view. Put him on a rack, or hang him up by his thumbs, and order him to change those ideas. He may verbally recant, but deep inside his viscera will be heard to murmur, "But that *is* how the world is. People *are* like that. Maybe I can change my views, but how can you change those people and the truth about the world?"

Fortunately, emotion and thinking are only two (of seven or eight) ways by which a person gains reality. And reality for money-making isn't either of these.

To show you what it is, let me use as an example a thread from a novel published a few years ago titled *Cash McCall*. At the beginning of the story, an old man on this particular morning arrives as usual at his factory. It is his own company, and for thirty years it and his work in it have been the joy of his life. But now, as he enters and looks over the familiar scene, he couldn't care less.

His factory manufactures, among other items, television shells— i.e., the cabinets; not the works but the wooden boxes that hold them. Each year he and his department heads engage in a terrific hassel over what is beautiful in a television cabinet. In fact, the top production and design men often come almost to blows as the hour of decision arrives. But our over-sixty owner has been the arbiter of these battles. He has held the creative people away from each others' throats, and it has been subjectively important for him to participate in these discussions and struggles.

This morning it has no interest for him. He wonders how he could ever have cared. Abruptly, he wants out.

Now, Cash McCall and his associates are the kind of people who buy up good businesses. When they hear that the factory is for sale, they ask the disgusted owner what he wants for it. In the book it says that our elderly manufacturer had never before wondered what his business might be worth. But now he does, and he comes up with a price of two million.

Find a Manager Who Has Quality Eight

Since McCall and his group have plans which transcend the cost of any one factory, they pay him his money without argument. But now they have a problem. They've got to find a man with qualities similar to those of the previous owner who can be put in charge of their newly purchased factory. They need someone who can arrive for work every morning with a feeling of strong interest in the problems of the day.

They don't have a business until they have such a man.

What is the ability that Mr. Manufacturer lost on that morning when he could no longer be interested in his factory and its activities? And that the new man must have?

It's not reasoning. The people who get into this couldn't-careless feeling can still solve problems and almost automatically observe the nature of the data they need. It's not emotion. People in this state have said to me, "I have a strong feeling I ought to be doing something. It's just—nothing has meaning for me any more."

So there you have it. The man that Cash McCall and his associates have to have is one who is still capable of putting meaning into objects and locations.

Such a man doesn't have that empty feeling. He thinks there is beauty in objects, a right place for a business, and that some things are more important than others.

If you are young and unalienated, the idea that anyone could ever be disillusioned (and that's not quite the right word) to that extent may be unbelievable. But that's what can happen to people who didn't know (as you probably don't) that there is no natural meaning in things.

Consider for a moment, what is beauty in a box that holds the machinery of television?

Things that we once thought beautiful soon lose their appeal. Cars of a few years ago, television sets, furniture and most other items seem to go through a cycle in our minds and appear to become uglier.

Instead, some current model of new design appeals to us.

A person who can create and maintain such reality seems to have a picture in his mind to which he can feed energy. It stimulates him. He becomes, and remains, enthusiastic. The energy thus focused puts beauty into a car or a television set, and life into a business, a profession, or an activity.

He creates reality that wasn't there before.

And as long as he does that, so long as he is stimulated into believing that what he is doing is worthwhile—that's a going business.

But the moment that he feels it's no longer important he starts to fail.

The irony of all this is that at some level he believes that things are meaningful.

What happens here is probably as important as any other subject in the world. A few years ago, *Time* Magazine had an article about successful men over forty who were beginning to falter. Apparently these men were appearing in ever greater numbers in the offices of psychiatrists. They wanted to know if there was any meaning to life.

Need for Meaning Not Relevant

Let me state right here. I am not planning to engage in a controversial philosophical argument about such matters. In this book we're not concerned with true reality—whatever that may be. But what I am describing is what happens to people.

You may be sure that when these men started they believed that out there in the world certain objects and activities had a meaning of their own. When the feeling of disillusionment begins—if it does—it means they have come by a roundabout way to the truth: that out there in the world are only dreams that other people have made come true.

At this point—like our aging manufacturer in *Cash McCall* —many people suffer an internal disaster. This doesn't have to happen. The truth is they always put the reality into the thing.

When I first had this picture, I wrote Mr. C., the youngest and financially most successful of the three men I have mentioned. He wrote back and said: "The main point is concentration, singleness of purpose, intensity of interest in what you're doing, one product for the manufacturer, one character for the writer."

Mr. C. was certainly describing Quality Eight—the creation of reality, being interested. That's where concentration comes from.

How to Regain Interest in Life in Two Steps

If you have no interest in anything, or had interest and lost it—that's one problem. If your interest is in something that makes no money—that's another.

I have a solution for both.

STEP ONE

For the first (no-interest) make duplicate cards with these words:

Today there is no change in my continuing feeling that life or _____ (write the name of an activity in which you were once engaged successfully) is meaningless.

Carry one of the duplicate cards with you. Paste the other one on your bedroom mirror or clothes closet door where you will see it first thing in the morning.

STEP TWO

For the second type (a no-money interest), also prepare duplicate cards. (Carry one, paste one in your room.) The message:

Today, I am still concentrating on making real _____ (write in the name of the no-money activity), which I anticipate will make me little or no money.

The messages on these cards are challenges—and something more. Confronted by a negative truth, the mind is reluctant to acknowledge it. Please don't think that simply being in this condition is a challenge, or is the same as confronting a verbalization of it. Confronting is an active facing of the fact.

If you merely feel the misery, or apathy, of it each day without actively confronting it, nothing will ever change. Face the actual fact—and the speed of the change may startle you.

Hypnotism and the Twelve Qualities

Is there a shortcut? What about hypnotism, that mysterious modality whereby somebody else verbally reaches past our defenses?

It would be nice if we could all be hypnotized and endowed with the dozen qualities, while at the same time the equal power of doubt and unreality was forever lulled.

Even if it were technically possible, statistically it cannot happen. There aren't enough practising hypnotists.

Recently, in recognizing hypnosis as a science useful as an aid to healing, the American Medical Association took the attitude that it should be used only by persons possessing proper degrees for specific therapeutic purposes. That limits the number of qualified hypnotists even more. In setting this limitation the A.M.A. in fact simply recognized limitations inherent in the method.

Hypnosis is technically a fairly well-understood phenomenon. Entirely aside from the fact that not everyone can be hypnotized, it has been observed that a percentage of hypnotic subjects progressively resist the mental control of any power other than their own consciousness. In addition, each person would probably require a slight variation in the wording it takes to make a suggestion acceptable to him.

From the foregoing, we may deduce that statistically speaking we shall not float through life with our doubts lulled by clouds of hypnotism and our desires enforced by positive suggestions.

However, if you do have a qualified hypnotist available, you might try hypnosis on Qualities Three and Eight and see what happens.

Do not use hypnotism on the other ten Qualities. Each of the others in its own way has an underlying psychic complexity which cannot, and should not, be solved by a simple directive.

Please heed that limitation.

Other Realities

Money is made by people who select a combination of molecules, or ideas, point them out to a prospect, and say, "Isn't that desirable?"

Money is seldom found in a philosophy about sex, or eating, or science (as such), or about gaining happiness through love of nature, or through adventure, or from emotion.

Of course, you can immediately indicate Hugh Hefner and his *Playboy* Magazine success *(sex),* and those publishers of pornography and semi-pornography *(sex);* and there's a prostitute mentioned by Dr. Greenwald in his psychiatric study, *Call Girl,* who received fees from over 90,000 men—which he considered a record.

Notice how few are the people who actually make the money in the foregoing.

And then there's mysticism, certainly a big business—for a small number of specially endowed persons.

And commercialized sport, involving—my estimate—less than a hundred thousand persons. (But how long can the athletes themselves keep it up? The golden years are few in number for even the greatest.)

So now what about all those people engaged in the production and preparation of food *(eating)?* These are the necessity level jobs. Here we find man from time immemorial crouching close to the soil, planting his seeds, harvesting the resultant crops, and for more ages than one cares to think selling them for a pittance —or, worse, for the benefit of a landlord.

Unquestionably, machines have improvthe lot of the farmer. Yet I'm told he still gets up at 4:30 A.M. (This is offset by the fact that he has the privilege of going to bed at 8 P.M.) If he abandons these ancient routines for himself, and hires people to do such things while he and his family live in town, or travel, then we have a different reality. The farm has become a symbol, a business. It will prosper, and he with it, to the exact extent that he can convert from the eating level of reality to the abstract level.

The transformation is not easy, and many an aspiring farmer has had to go back to ploughing because he didn't know how to manage his farm as a business.

In that comparison we have the difference between modern money-making reality, and the historical primitive realities of man frantically tearing a meager living out of the soil.

Such things have their own solidity, and it is hard for the mass of individuals involved to expand their thoughts about them to a more abstract level. Any work which derives from mysticism, or sex, or eating, has at the production level very little money in it. The laborer has been virtually a slave, and has had to fight his ruthless and greedy oppressors for every ounce lifted off his burden. And for the vast majority, mysticism is something for which they pay; even those who receive the money, with few exceptions live a life of self-denial.

There is a feeling in a percentage of people that someone is to blame for all this. They accordingly become alienated from our society and refuse to create forward-going reality.

Alienated people are a form of waste. And essentially there is no future in wasting. Peter W. is an interesting example.

The Money Personality Shapes the Real World with His Own Intense Beliefs

A few years ago, Peter W. won over $20,000 on a national TV show. In about a year he was broke. He thereupon tried to blackmail the producer on the grounds that he had been illegally coached in answering the questions that had won him the money. When the producer refused to pay, Peter W. talked to the press. And that was the end of that popular program.

Many persons with a $20,000 nest egg would have used it as

capital for the beginning of a fortune. Peter W. blew that amount in 14 months.

On the other hand, Silas Y. inherited approximately $8,000 when he was 26. He married his childhood sweetheart and the two of them set up a printing shop with a part of the money, and gradually developed a business which is today worth several hundred thousand dollars.

What quality did Silas Y. have that Peter W. did not have? Silas had the ability to make normal, everyday need abstractions real. Peter did not.

We should never completely write off a person who, for any reason, was able to get hold of twenty thousand dollars. He may have a distorted version of Quality Eight, which may someday stand him in good stead. But Peter W. has a lot of twisted energy to get control of before he can ever settle down into an ordinary channel of moneymaking, where—by the way—the most money is to be made. Yes, the ordinary, everyday affairs of mankind, where the real needs are, are the source of the fabulous fortunes that have been and are being made in this country.

To illustrate how this all fits, let's consider what happened to Mr. C. Some years ago Mr. C., then a young man of 25, was struck down by polio. With his life saved by the Nurse Kenny method, he slowly recovered the use of his limbs—but he was also a changed man.

As he described it to me, "I had a lot of time to think over the timid kind of life I had lived up to that illness. And so I decided that from now on I'm going to stop being afraid of rejection. I'm going to go forward as if it's all right for me to be alive, and I'm going to live like a man who has grown up."

Fifteen years after that decision he was getting a salary of $150,000 a year plus a huge expense account, and later he got a piece of the action (40 per cent).

If only we could all do what Mr. C. did: a single decision *at the feeling level*—and the job was done.

But it took a siege of polio, which almost killed him, to build up that feeling to the necessary intensity. Then he decided effortlessly.

Alas, this is not a practicable solution for the rest of us. Many people make personality changes when they are ill. Most of these decisions are in the direction of fear, not—as was C's—away from it.

People who are near death all too often acquire a feeling of no personal worth. Mr. C.'s brush with death, on the other hand, made him reject the negative values he had previously put on himself in relation to the successful people he knew at that time, who somehow had more right—it seemed to him up to that time—to have the good things of this world. He began at once to inject that newly acquired conviction of self-worth into whatever he did.

If your interest in your own future well-being is intense enough, you can put meaning into such abstractions as restaurants, stores, apartment buildings, or vacant lots. The abstraction will come to life and make money in proportion to the reality you have attached to it.

Meaning into Moneymaking

The money personality puts meaning into activities that make money. Putting meaning into something can be a severe aberration. It can become a type of paranoia where almost everything is a signal. Observing this type of paranoid person, we can learn more about the mechanism of creating reality.

The unfortunate victim of the mental disease that is involved projects meaning into an object. *Example:* The old lady who sees a movie ad and is convinced that Gregory Peck loves her. *Another example:* The way his meals are served telegraphs to a man that his food is being poisoned by the F.B.I.

The way a glass is set on a table, a curtain drawn, trash put into the garbage, the color of clothing which someone is wearing —all are signals which, often, he does not quite understand but which he never doubts have a sinister meaning.

The people who have this illness present a stereotype of behavior which does not vary widely over thousands of cases. From such similarities we may deduce that an actual brain mechanism is involved in the attribution of meaning to things.

It seems to be a specific line, or channel, which is somehow in a very twisted condition. But the twist essentially produces the same phenomenon.

Interesting, eh?

It would seem that attributing meaning is something we are born to do. An overlying conditioning occurs, yes. We think like the culture we live in, or resist it in varying degrees. But we have no alternative to doing *something* in this area. The channel is there. It has to be used to create sane, un-sane, or insane reality.

When we observe the average person in relation to his environment, we discover in him many destructive thoughts. These are not at the psychotic level that I have just described; what they do establish is that the individual has sat in judgment on the society in which he lives and has found it wanting. The number of people who do this is far larger than one might suspect. Most of it comes under the heading of unwillingness to conform.

At the extreme of this normal alienation, the person will not play the game of our economy. His attitude is one of total contempt and disgust. He wouldn't, in a manner of speaking, be caught dead in a situation where anybody might suspect him of being interested in a money-making scheme.

What he is making real are his reasons for his alienation. The mere idea of opening an ordinary store or operating a restaurant, or something "cruddy" like that, arouses all the antagonism he feels for the culture into which he was born.

There are less extreme versions of alienation than the foregoing. But here also we all too often find not the lack of ability, but varying degrees of refusal to apply it where it will do some good.

Since in this book we're only concerned with the kind of person you have to be to make money, my point is: To the extent that you can overcome alienation and make something that has money potentialities in it important to yourself, to that extent you will be able to make money.

And, remember! the reality is not in the *thing.* It is in *you.* The thing, the location, the idea, is a piece of blah. It has no meaning until you focus your life energy upon it.

Occupations That Make Money

How can a person start to make combinations of molecules and ideas desirable first of all to himself and then to a buying public? In short, how can he (you) make something important out of, say, a vacant lot?

There are people who, seeing a piece of unoccupied land, say, "Boy, wouldn't that be a good location for a restaurant!" And they promptly work up the enthusiasm of others, get the money and build one.

Take a look at what enthuses you: Parties. Girls (boys). Music. Reading. Watching TV or movies. Drag racing, golf, swimming, fixing old cars in your back yard, playing bridge, surfing.

They're not it, of themselves. Your skill at some of them *could* be used to analyze your ability a la Quality Five.

Or is it the following: Are you studying to be a doctor, engineer, certified accountant, scientist, or lawyer? These are the top professions. (But many businessmen do better.)

As a group the very top professional people are medical doctors, though dentists are coming up fast and because of the more stable hours may actually have a better deal.

Other things with money potentiality that you could be doing or learning are:

. . . The details of real estate, figuring out how to buy land or a house . . . Noticing that auto service businesses, manufacturers of almost anything (even on a small scale), builders and building repair service are usually well-to-do . . . Noticing that learning any science properly, or any technology, or even a mechanical or artistic craft, can provide a good basic income.

Those and other similar activities relating to needs—they're it. Make one of those things real. How?

The method is by way of the Rule Eight card (1) which will directly challenge your present no-interest or little-money interest, and (2) which by confronting you repeatedly with your present attitude and unmeaningful situation will alter it automatically (because that's the way the mind responds to an exactly true statement of a condition).

The Difference Between Rule Five and Rule Eight

So what's the difference between Rule Eight and Rule Five? Let's place them next to each other for comparison:

RULE FOR ACHIEVING QUALITY FIVE

Ask yourself:
(1) In what you're planning, is there any money? (2) Am I now the type of person who can make money in that area (business)?

RULE FOR ACHIEVING QUALITY EIGHT

Today, I am still concentrating on making real _____ [activity] from which I anticipate making little or no money.

See the difference. Five is a caution against getting involved in a no-money activity. Eight is a method of getting you to be aware of your present no-money (or no interest) situation.

Five says think through what you're going to do in the future. Eight makes you aware of what you have been making important and challenges its value.

For example, if you are now making real somebody else's ideas, by looking at Rule Eight repeatedly you soon will be bound to notice that it's mostly for his benefit. Only now you won't be able to be resentful about it, because each morning as you look at Rule Eight you re-affirm your decision to continue putting importance into his purposes. There's nothing wrong with working for someone else while you're getting started, but in the long run it's wise only if he shares with you more of the benefits.

But it's your choice—which *you* can change by the use of Rule Eight.

If "he" is a big company, you'll have to figure out (Quality Five) now to use your pay as a steppingstone to affluence in your spare time. If he is a small firm, your Quality Five reasoning could take into account the possibility that a little extra enterprise could lead straight to a junior partnership or equivalent.

Make that real for yourself—and for him.

It's up to you. It's always up to you.

There are no unqualified riders.

The Essence of Quality Eight: Focusing Your Life

Focusing pure, going-forward *doingness* on a business or occupation—that's Quality Eight. If you guide your motion with the good sense from Five, enhance it with the automatic profit response of Quality Three, and defend it with the non-victim posture of Quality One, you will have an intense integration of the principal money-making forces.

Not all energies of nature and life are pure in the sense that I am describing. Many become too violent, go out of control, and rapidly trap themselves into a more stable (static) form. This is part of the law of conservation of energy. A heated object soon cools. An explosive object explodes and its elements so unite with the atmosphere and the soil that no further explosion can take place.

And so a stone that was once a flaming molten mass in a seething volcano now lies cold and hard on a hillside. Its available energy is in its dead weight. Similarly, a violent criminal is soon caged and his movments restricted.

During the Great Depression a young man was hired by the parents of a friend of mine to mow the lawn and do a little weed pulling. At the time, the going rate for such work was as low as 15¢ an hour, up to as high as 40¢—but these people always paid 75¢ an hour.

After two hours' work, the young man came to the door and demanded $5.00. Offered the usual generous $1.50, he threatened to invoke the law. The woman of the house promptly called the police. He thereupon negotiated $2.00 from her and departed, muttering threats. He was long gone by the time a police officer finally put in appearance.

This young man was angry at a society that failed to provide employment. There's nothing wrong with that, because any strong emotion is often a good basis for making a thought real. But somehow he felt that people who were not down where he was, were more responsible for the depression than he was. So he failed to take proper advantage of an opportunity for work. All he needed in those days when a dime bought a quart of milk or a loaf of bread was a few customers a week for his lawn-mowing services, and he would have been able to meet his minimum expenses.

But his attitude was "going against" (attack) when it should have been "going toward." If you own a business, or run one, and you are a "going against" person, stay in the back of the building out of sight.

His attack probably needed to be directed against another target—that is, against slow government response in that area to the problems created by the Great Depression. This is only a "probably," since it is a matter of opinion as to what should be done in any area against an all-pervasive depression.

How responsible was the householder for the hard times? That would also be a matter of opinion, wouldn't it, and not of settled truth? But an interesting sidelight to this particular incident was the following: These people had come to this continent from Europe. During his first winter in North America, the man of the house had earned the family's entire food and shelter by walking with a shovel from house to house and hiring himself out to clean walks. This was a "going toward" action, and this man was soon on his way to a prosperity that enabled him to pay, when he didn't have to, 75¢ an hour for yardwork.

What am I saying? I'm saying that our over-aggressive young man had enough intensity of anger in him to make the abstraction of social justice real for himself.

Personal Consequences of the Great Depression

As we know, since we can look back, the Great Depression stirred nations as well as individuals. Dynamic forces were unleashed: in this country, the potent "going toward" New Deal; in Europe, the destructive "going against" power of Nazism. In Asia was another "going against"; the Japan of that time moved with mighty armies into China and Manchuria. These two victim areas, feeling themselves too weak to resist, tried to avoid a direct confrontation with the attacker. The ferment of intense emotion created by these and other actions began in the early thirties and presently built up to the greatest war in human history.

But the lawn-mowing young man, in attempting to force by threat *one* person to accept his opinions on the matter of responsibility for what he was suffering in the world-shaking depression, and to fork over, was close to blackmail—i.e., to a criminal act.

In his action, he distorted the qualities necessary to the making of money. He was so determined not to be a victim that he had moved over to the level of attempting to be a victimizer. He had a reason for charging a profit which was unacceptable to his customer. And it would be an exaggeration to call his attempt to extract $5.00 a well-thought-out money-making scheme a la Quality Five.

However, let's not lose sight of one fact: our young man actually had a lot of Quality Eight. Twisted though it was, he was putting out strength. And he did collect $2.00 before departing, and did make a lasting impression. What he did can be likened to a high-pressure salesman who puts everything he has into one pitch; he's not planning to come back this way.

That young man proved once more that *anybody* who has a good supply of Quality Eight, no matter how distorted, can make *some* money.

Thoughts May Dim Your Desire

I have a couple of additional thoughts about Eight, and then I'll let it go.

Number One: Many people as they grow older, like our over-60 manufacturer in *Cash McCall,* begin to lose interest in making money. They are brought to a no-desire state by the feeling that life really has no meaning. The image of the grave intrudes and makes nothing of their previous goals. Why—they ask—run to the cemetery when you can walk and take a little longer?

As I've already indicated, the situation is much worse than such late-thinkers on the subject realize. *There never was any meaning in a thing.* A human being looked at the thing, and projected from an energy source inside him the reality necessary to give an object the meaning that made it attractive and worthwhile.

Thought Number Two: How can we take a person out of this dwindling spiral of apathy in connection with the certainty of death?

Are you waiting eargerly for my answer?

It is not to be found in religion. Religious leaders are the first to point out that things of the world are as nothing beside the love of God. Hundreds of years ago, the Jesuits in their recruiting argument lured a likely prospect down a path of logic, whereby he progressively agreed that only total service to Jesus was meaningful. The method of reasoning used has ever since been called Jesuitic logic.

No matter what the cause, watch out for this kind of logic. It can lead you to a lifetime of making real the anguish of wearing a hair shirt or some equivalent.

With that non-money-making alternative in mind, let me now propose a more palatable solution. Be like Mr. C. Stop being a coward. Cease that wretched trembling. Walk slowly to the grave, yes, but don't crawl. Live as if you will never die until you actually step into your coffin.

9

Ninth Quality of the Money Personality: Giving Generously

The money personality gives, in order to turn himself into, or maintain himself as, a mature adult.

The giving of gifts could be a major therapy for your purse.

If you are not a gift giver, I want you to consider making a switchover for the benefit of your bank account.

It could be that you are a person who craves to *receive* gifts. If you are, it might be of interest to you to know what aspect of *that* craving is all right and what isn't (in relation to your becoming a moneymaker—which of course is all we are concerned with in this book).

Am I *opposed* to people receiving gifts? No, no, no! The receipt of money or other valuable objects as gifts, or in any other safe way, never of itself hurt anyone, regardless of the origin.

Using and Misusing Gifts

As a young man, Howard Hughes inherited a portion of the Hughes Tool Company of Texas, his share then being worth about $450,000—at least so I have read. He parlayed his gift (inheritance) into a reported 450 *million.*

Sure didn't hurt him in terms of making money to receive a gift of wealth, did it?

However, as many a would-be heir has discovered, it often takes mom and dad an unconscionable long time to kick off and so enable their darling to receive that kind of gift.

What I'm saying is that the number of individuals at any given time who could use a gift (inheritance or other kind) far exceeds the present available supply.

Each year, millions of people find themselves either without an income or with one that has been reduced. In eras not long past, their only recourse in times of emergency was to turn to friends or relatives for the gifts or loans needed to tide them over. Some of the people thus aided used the money, and the time gained thereby, to the end of finding another self-supporting source of income. Others either not so fortunate, or careless or unthinking, found themselves finally with the money gone, needing additional gifts. There was a time in history when such persons suffered the most severe personal disasters after they had exhausted all possible resources of gift income; and in many parts of the world such a condition still prevails.

Today in the United States the individual who loses a job, or for some reason comes to a state of acute financial distress, can usually obtain unemployment compensation from the State as an initial buffer. This is not a gift. It is insurance for which he paid a part of his salary while he worked. This carries him for many months, but it does eventually end. If he still lacks an income he is now entitled to seek welfare assistance. In the larger cities, such additional aid is generously available.

We may eventually come to a semi-Utopia (not too far from now, really) in which everyone receives a basic income from the State as a gift whether or not he works.

In my opinion we are well advised to do this in order to eliminate the costly supervision of our top-heavy welfare systems, with all the effort wasted on it by capable people who could be spending their time more usefully than wearily doing the endless repetitive chores involved.

If this is already advisable, then obviously the receipt of money is not of itself a bad thing.

Where it is a problem (and it is), that problem derives from the individual himself—you!

You may have a "thing" on giving, accepting, making, holding, having, or receiving money.

That may not be so important when we all finally are entitled to that annual income from our government. But it is important now.

Deciding Each Day to Be Poor—or Rich

The subject has been intensively examined by other persons than myself.

In France there lives at this writing an unusually brilliant egg-head named Jean-Paul Sartre. During World War II, Sartre developed a new philosophy which he named Existentialism—which has as its key the idea that even when you sit absolutely still, you are making a choice; in sitting, you *choose* to do nothing.

If you are on welfare (according to this theory), you choose to be taken care of by other persons. You make this choice minute by minute during all your waking hours each day, says Sartre.

The same truth applies to any other low-level, little-money activity in which you are engaged.

You may believe that what you do is something you hardly ever think about; it's so automatically a part of your life that it seldom even crosses your mind. "No," argues existentialist theory. "Each morning when you wake up your very first act is a reaffirmation of your choice. If you are on welfare, you turn lazily over in bed, or rise leisurely, or do something similar. The one thing you don't do is get up with the *intention* of changing your way of life—*this morning*. That would be a choice of another color."

In the same way, if you hold some low-pay job, you get up and prepare to go to that job—again. Ordinarily (for multi-millions) no other plan is even considered.

Why?

Why don't you move to act more effectively, to do better—*now;*
to become involved in the market place in a way that counts?
There's a reason.

We all begin life wholly dependent.

If the individual's environment is friendly, and if the life situations that confront him are not too difficult, and *if* his parents
show a certain amount of good sense in meeting his emotional
needs—then he will grow up to an average level of self-sufficiency.
That is, he will be able to shift any dependency on his mother to
his wife, and on his father to his boss or buddy. Society considers
such a person mature.

If, on the contrary, the individual's environment and his responses to life situations overstimulated his dependency tendencies, he remains emotionally and mentally immature. This condition, which exists to some extent in all of us, in some individuals
is present in an extreme way, yet it may not be visible except in
a philosophy of wanting something for nothing, or in an attitude
which cannot even conceive of having possessions beyond the
want level.

Turning Your Attention Toward Others

Sartre, the Existentialist philosopher, states that a gift (a giving
of an object of value) is an act of destruction.

The average recipient of a gift feels that he can use that kind
of destruction from now until doomsday. But a gift, for the most
part, is the tiniest drop in the bucket of what a person needs
merely to remain alive in our high-priced economy. So we need
to consider its true role, and can do so without its loss or gain
becoming a trauma.

Let us first dispose of the penny-pinching (extreme non-victim)
type who—according to reports—would let his poor old mother
starve. Is such an example of miserly wealth a proof of anything?
What it probably proves is that all you need are some of the
qualities that I am describing here. Sufficiently intensified, even
a few suffice for money making.

However, if you are a tightwad, please note first if it has actually gotten you somewhere. Do you have an ample supply of the green stuff? If you haven't, the time has come for you to become a gift giver.

The doors of the world open to the person (man or woman) who comes bearing a gift.

For the person who has neglected this magical method, and who now at my urging engages in it, there are at least four (count 'em) great rewards. First, and most important, he presently breaks forever the craving he has had since childhood to be a receiver of gifts.

(Please note: This does not remove all his childhood behavior from the adult; just the part that has to do with moneymaking. Which after all is what we are concerned with here.)

Second, of equal value to him is his gradual discovery that people assume goodwill on the part of a gift giver. This of course *should* be, and presently (except in the case of a few people who are just too snakey to change) *will* be the case.

There are people who are so subjective, and have such a need to receive gifts, that they will probably never repay the giver with any spontaneous offering of their own. But most people will. So in the long run the giver receives equal value in one way or another. (Reward Number Three.)

The feeling of trust that recipients of gifts eventually feel for the giver can lead to many things. In a business situation, if they can do something for you, they will. 'Nuf said. (And that's Reward Four.)

Be sure, of course, never to betray such a trust. Never be greedy in connection with what is offered you in this way. Assume that time will take care of you better than any momentary opportunism, regardless of a few tightwads and victimizers whose tactics seem to be successful.

What you get back in return for gifts is totally beside the point. Your gift-giving is for *you*. What it does for the other person, or brings back from him, is virtually immaterial.

You must *change* whatever in *you* prevents you from being a gift giver. When you have become a giver of gifts, you will have made a decisive transformation in your own being—something on the colossal order of casting off a vital portion of the lingering disease of childhood dependence. Getting well in this department will include your becoming mature.

Can you imagine receiving a greater gift than that—ever?

In this analogy the *giving* of the gift is the medicine.

Gifts and Status

There are, of course, other aspects to gift giving and receiving. For example, there is the person who demands a gift, or expects it. What is his status?

When the Roman general Pompey, still only a beardless youth and too young to be admitted to the Senate, arrived in Rome fresh from his triumphs in North Africa, he demanded a reception befitting a military conqueror. Sulla, the dictator, refused him, saying that he was too young. Pompey's proud answer was that more people worshipped rising suns than setting suns, implying that his sun was rising and the elderly Sulla's setting. Sulla, a great man, was amused by this remark and generously granted Pompey the triumphant reception he demanded.

Pompey's expectation of a reward for good services shows the spirit of the natural man of power.

Similarly, the salesman who knows his power not only sells more, but also demands and gets the highest commissions. The rising executive, who deserves a gift, often asks for a raise. Such a gift, or raise, should be his company's way of showing that it appreciates good work. A company which doesn't present good people with this type of gift—which is in a way, for the executive, a share of the profits which he has earned for the firm—will quickly (on the average) lose such a man to a managerial group that knows about such methods of paying for merit.

In giving earned gifts to a few persons, the wise management also presents smaller, and not necessarily earned, gifts to their other employees. This is to prevent dissatisfaction and to build morale. It is true, employees come to expect such bonuses as their due; so if it's been a bad year, and there are not going to be such gifts, a certain amount of employee relations communication is in order.

Coming back to the personal level, *you,* the best gift for you to present is a thoughtful, suitable item, tailored to the individual. Give any good little thing—a bottle of liquor for those who imbibe or entertain, chocolates, or flowers, or a book. A quickly proffered cigarette to a person who smokes is surely a small but appreciated way to be generous.

Keep your eyes open for inexpensive gift potentials: an unusual looking ballpoint pen, or a record to suit the other person's musical tastes.

I recommend that you begin your gift-giving career by taking something (e.g., a bottle of wine) to the host and hostess *whenever* in the future you are invited somewhere.

The main idea is this: for *your* sake, take a gift. Present it with a cheerful smile.

In your entire life henceforth, give gifts without thought of return.

Finally—do not confuse gifts with donations to the needy. Do that also, but be aware that that's another part of the forest.

Ultimate Afterthought

A gift to your girlfriend is not a gift in the meaning of this chapter.

10

Tenth Quality of the Money Personality: Becoming Sensitive to Signals

The money personality recognizes signals of success or failure.

All the little fishes in a particular spot in the ocean skidoo madly when a long shadow suddenly darkens the water above them.

In doing so, they respond to a signal from their environment. The long shadow is that of a big fish who eats unwary little fishes for breakfast, lunch and dinner. Naturally, in such an ecology, somebody has to pay the price, and the big fishes usually gobble one or two or more of the little guys on every foray.

But if you're a little fish, and you beat it if the water even looks dark for a moment, then your chances of becoming a bigger fish improve with every day that passes.

Increasing Your Awareness of Signals

The world of people is a lot like that. Usually, loss or threat of loss casts its shadow before it, perhaps more subtly. But the message is there for the person who can heed it.

Among humans, the signal can take many forms. A warning type can be a change in the attitude of your employer. He's less friendly. If you are capable of evaluating all the factors in such a reaction from him, then it might be advisable for you to batten down the hatches on new expenses at home, start saving larger percentages of your next few salary checks, and get ready to look for another job.

A far more common signal is the kind that issues from a piece of expensive machinery: you hear an odd sound in your car. The advice of all good signal-perceivers is, as soon as possible after hearing it, drive in to see your auto mechanic. Have him make a check. He may catch the problem before it becomes an expensive repair job.

On the other hand, opportunity may be knocking. At a party, a pretty girl suddenly looks into your eyes, and then quickly looks away again. Male operators—sometimes called wolves—tell me that a look of this kind is a signal that your attentions are welcome.

Naturally, the signals we are concerned with in this book are those that either warn you that a storm is brewing in your financial affairs, or nudge you toward a moneymaking opportunity.

The first thing we observe about a signal is that you have to have knowledge to understand what it is. And you even have to have knowledge to understand that there has been a signal at all.

A friend of mine, while taking a trip through rural Mexico, stopped at a small farm, and discovered that the farmer's greatest sadness had to do with the fact that his little radio didn't work any more. My friend examined the instrument and discovered that the batteries were dead. He replaced them with the batteries from his own set. The radio was immediately back in working order. The farmer was delighted. What was more, he now knew for the first time that the gradual reduction of the radio's efficiency (as the batteries ran down) was a signal from the instrument that something would soon have to be done.

Every individual in a highly sophisticated society like ours has literally thousands of spcialized bits of information whereby he can receive, detect, and identify signals—and either act, or not act, depending on his purposes.

Signals to Heed in Businesses Big and Small

If you are in business, or you have a job, you are continually receiving signals that you should be listening to or perceiving with your other senses. And you are also sending forth signals that your superiors will be taking note of (if you work for someone else), or your customers and employees (if you work for yourself).

Not too long ago, the man who had been put in charge of a subsidiary company of a large organization began to tell his friends that he detected weaknesses in the until-then superman who headed the main organization, and that he was seeking another post before the deluge. These words came to the ears of the great man, who quickly took a sharp look at his actions (which may have stimulated such a view of him) and promptly corrected himself. Within a few weeks, the first man ceased his anxious talk and settled back into his job, even turning down another offer.

Both men in this situation are entitled to five stars for their sensitivity to and response to signals of failure.

In another instance, a company comptroller kept advising *his* super-boss that income flow was faltering. The sums that were coming in during this faltering period were so vast it was difficult even for an experienced management to realize that the proverbial handwriting was indeed beginning to show faintly on the wall, and that it wasn't just a normal business downswing.

The big boss had his own game-playing ways of dealing with certain situations. In this instance, he made a couple of tentative requests for loans ranging from six to thirty million dollars. To his shocked dismay, the banks were reluctant to talk to him *on any terms.* At last alerted, he ceased his merry round of traveling and pleasure, and began to show up at the office at six A.M. In his early days, he had handled *all* top level hiring himself, but for a few years now he had delegated this task to a trusted aide. So as a starter he talked personally to every high level executive, drawing out each man and listening for those scores of little signals by which he judged leadership material.

Obviously, such men intuitively look for the twelve qualities that I am describing in this book. Some men give them other names. Others just *feel* their presence in terms of quantity and intensity.

The top businessman soon discovered that his otherwise very able aide had brought in friends and relatives, and that the real purpose for so doing was not to find the right man for the particular job but to set up an empire within the organization.

It was pretty late for unscrambling all those eggs, but he began by beating the financial bushes in earnest, so to speak, and persuaded a distant bank to loan him three and a half million; then another bank came through with six and a half. This staved off immediate disaster. Then he did two things inside the company: dislodged unsuitable executives as swiftly and gently as possible, and exercised escape clauses in contracts with agencies that represented his company in the major cities across the land—agencies which, according to the comptroller, operated below the standard of excellence by which this firm had gained its initial leadership in its field.

During this entire period, sharp observers had been driving down this company's stock on the market. (If you've ever wondered why stocks go down, here's one example, and why they go up—that's what began to happen again.) The men at the head of the large companies *naturally* have enough of the twelve qualities I am describing, and naturally select top management help with similar qualities. The moment that somebody who has other motives gets into top level personnel selection, the decline of the company begins at that instant.

I am indebted for the foregoing examples to Mr. B. and Mr. C. And the lesson that you should learn from them is that even up there the same passions are at work as down where most people function.

At the very, very top it's the man who can make things real who is successful in that vast fashion. In order to do so, he had *better* be able to hear the signals of both failure and success. And—more important—when he hears them he must be able to act before it is too late.

The Signals Known to Millions

If you were an Indian living in the American wilderness 330 years ago, then your knowledge and associations, and the signals to which you responded, related to survival in that primitive world.

Today, if you have lived anywhere in North America or Western Europe, your associations, and the signals to which you have learned to respond, are from the world as it is now.

So you are entitled to ask in a tone of mild disappointment: Are they that local? Are signals really so closely related to individual human experience? Is there nothing basic?

The answers to the first two questions are yes, they are local, and yes, they are related to individual human experience; but to that needs to be added the further, important thought that the experience and localization are shared by millions. Thus, the same signals have similar meanings in any given period of history.

Fortunately or unfortunately—you decide—the answer to question three is yes, there is something so basic to human response to signals that it will just about lift you out of your chair when I tell you what it is.

Learning How Fatigue Affects Signal Sensitivity

In the early days of Communism there lived in Russia a physiologist by the name of Pavlov. Pavlov is world-famous in psychological and other scientific circles for his experiments with ringing bells while dogs ate their meals.

A typical Pavlovian experiment: The dog was fed; the bell was rung. Then one day the bell rang but no food was offered. The dog salivated anyway just as if there was food. Pavlov called the reaction a conditioned reflex. The dog had come to associate the food with the ringing of a bell.

I find Pavlov a hard man to like. He never asked why Stalin was interested first in these conditioning experiments and later with the less-well-known fatigue experiments financed by the Soviet government. He was the pure scientist who had no concern with what was done with his discoveries after they were published.

What was done with his fatigue experiments was that they became the basis for first Russian, and then Chinese Communist brainwashing. And that is related to signals in a way that will chill every bone in your body.

But it is also very enlightening, and may have a personal message for you.

This *real* brainwashing—which I have described extensively in my novel, *The Violent Man*—consists of requiring *all* the people in the country, after they have returned from their day's labors and after giving them bare minutes to eat their evening meal, to report to the local meeting place and there engage in grueling hours of self-criticism. Midnight comes, and everybody is still there, exhausted, sleepy; and still the remorseless Party Liners (who know exactly what they're doing) keep each bone-weary person at the task of self-examination and self-criticism in relation to—you've guessed it—how good a Communist he is or has been.

At 2 A.M. everybody is finally allowed to go home. But of course these are workers, and they barely get their eyes shut for a wink or two before it's dawn and time to go to work, where things aren't easy either.

That evening the same grueling hours of self-criticism are required. And the next day, and so on. Presently, the first physiologic change takes place.

The Three Stages of Fatigue

What Pavlov discovered with his dogs, and Stalin verified when he used the method to get confessions from prisoners, was that there are three stages of fatigue.

In the first stage, the victim becomes virtually unaware of stimuli (i.e., signals) from the environment. You may have heard the joke about the man who was going to train a mule. His first act was to pick up a two-by-four and with it to hit the mule a terrific whack across the shoulders. A horrified bystander protested at such cruelty. The farmer was surprised, and said in astonishment, "Before you can train a mule, you have to attract his attention."

That is just about the condition of the person who has been subjected to Pavlov's first stage of fatigue. You can speak to him, and he does not even turn his head. You can give him absolutely vital information about his survival, and it does not penetrate. He actually needs some variation of a whack with a two-by-four to get him to notice that somebody is talking to him.

It should immediately occur to you as it did to me—when I learned of these fatigue techniques—that, as we look around our world, we observe everywhere a very large number of persons who are insensitive to a vast range of signals. They need loud whacks to attract their attention. They have to have people explain things many times. They drive around in clanking cars and do not hear the clank, and downrate any advice about how dangerous it is to drive on tires that are shrunk to their bare skins.

For the record, this is the category that I belonged in, and to my credit I noticed it long before I ever read about Pavlov's experiments. I used to say to people, "Now, listen, I've discovered that a tremendous number of things go on around me that I don't see. So for God's sake, grab my arm, squeeze hard to get my attention, and then spell out for me the fact that something is happening, and what it is."

The second stage of fatigue, as Pavlov meticulously observed, is an exact reversal of the first. The affected individual scarcely notices the loud sounds and the huge light flashes. But he becomes intensely aware of small signals.

Now, before I tell you what the third fatigue signal is (as Pavlov observed it), permit me to offer my speculation as to why people not subjected to formal fatiguing techniques can exist in large numbers in our society.

The common denominator that I observed was in persons who had experienced high fever in an illness. I would guess from this that a severe rise in body temperature affects the brain in a similar way to fatigue; and, depending on how long the fever lasts, puts the victim through either the first, second, or third stage of fatigue-equivalence.

Innumerable childhood illnesses have these high-fever reactions. Thus we may speculate that the average man brings his ability to respond to signals with him out of the mists of childhood, and he never knew anything better. Never knew—until he reads these lines—that he had been deprived of an ability. And never did anything about it.

Well, ladies and gentlemen, the time has come.

However, before I tell you what to do, here is the third and final stage of the fatigue response as observed in countless experiments by Pavlov, and practiced upon countless victims by Stalin and Mao Tse-tung.

In the third fatigue stage, the person who is being tortured by being kept awake (the usual method), or forced to stand for hours holding both arms above his head (which was one of the principal methods of Russian secret police interrogators), does another and different inversion.

In both previous stages he resisted the falsehood that his villainous captors tried to force on him. For example, in Russia the police wanted him to confess that he had been a secret agent of Hitler, and had sabotaged production in his factory. He was totally innocent, so he resisted this accusation. But at the third stage of fatigue, he suddenly agrees. He signs a confession. He lists a long career of treasonable actions. He agrees that other persons whose names have been given him by his interrogator were involved with him.

Observing him do this, we may say that these quote third degree end-quote methods broke his spirit; that he knows better, but it doesn't matter any more. Yet it is not impossible, according to experts, that he now actually believes in the crimes to which he has confessed. Only a few persons recanted. The others went almost eagerly forward to their deaths.

On the dog level, Pavlov noted that at this third fatigue stage a dog turned against his former master and attached himself to his torturer.

So that's the picture, in brief. The human third-fatigue-stage subjects got palsy-walsy with *their* torturers; the dogs with theirs. It has the look of being more than just a broken spirit. Something basic has happened.

I have not looked too hard for this person's natural equivalent in our environment. I might tentatively wonder: could it be that yes-men and other over-agreeable persons (super-level—including certain but not all female-role homosexuals) fit in here?

I somehow don't want to consider this third-stage person. My feeling: he's beyond the reach of the technology of this chapter, though all the rest of the book is for him. Which is enough, for the most part.

So now what do we do?

Surviving in a World of Many Signals

Dealing with signals is a little bit like the victim/non-victim thing: once you become aware of the condition, you find yourself noticing it more—and more—and more.

So, right away, now that you have read these two chapters, you have that greater awareness going for you. Surely, you'll never completely forget what I have just told you about Pavlov's fatigue experiments, and about the three stages of fatigue and their symptoms.

Here are some of the things you can do.

One man to whom I described this quality said right away, "I'm a stage one fatigue-equivalent, and my wife is either stage two or she's just enormously noticing."

(I blessed him silently for having the sharp awareness that enabled him to use the information instantly, and admired him for being one of those people who don't engage in that tiresome ego-defense reaction by which so many individuals maintain an illusion against all the evidence: "Oh - no - nothing - like - that - ever - happened - to - me—Oh - yes - I - had - fever - but - it - didn't - affect - me - at - all - for - as - you - can - see - here - I - am - perfect - though - I - have - no - money.")

The first man—the one I blessed—was alert from that moment

on to his wife's awareness of small signals. Previously, he had downrated her reactions. Now, he listened when she "exaggerated"—that was the term he had formerly, silently, used to describe to himself what she did.

He still could not accept *all* her awarenesses. Since he examined everything she said with his reasoning brain, this suggests to me that her sensitivity was a stage two fatigue-equivalent and therefore not wholly rational. But she was pretty good.

A recent example: He told me that after a heavy wind, she said, "That tree at the corner of the house is going to blow down one of these windy days if we don't have the top cut off."

After thinking about why that might happen—they lived on a hillside, the tree grew in fill and not in the original soil—he called a tree-cutting service. When the next great wind came, two neighbors commended him for his foresight. As the tree grew taller, they had become worried also, but of course had been reluctant to offer advice.

From the foregoing, we may deduce this: Notice your own signal response. Look around to see if there is someone close by, preferably a member of your family, who can supplement what you can do.

It could be that between the two of you you can span the signal spectrum of success and threats to success.

Signals Perceived by Scaredy-Cats

Of course there's another side. A second man said to me, "My wife is an alarmist. She's got disaster on the brain. Every little thing makes her heart go pitty-pat with terror that something horrible is going to happen. So far it hasn't."

This woman's husband spoke to me at a lecture, and of course I had to admit that there were alarmist-types. That after all the stage two fatigue-equivalence was not a normal condition, and sensitivity to small signals could get out of hand. "However, in relation to success," I said to him, "it could be that the measure of who is more right, you or your wife, is how much money and property do you have?"

He admitted he had very little.

So regardless of whether or not she was an alarmist, he needed to take stock of himself and of her on a number of the qualities I have been describing, and not merely in connection with signals.

When *I* became aware of the signal thing, I personally started carrying a card with the following words on it:

SIGNAL RULE

Today, up to now, are there any signals that I have ignored?

All Signals Are Received by Everyone

Please notice, I say "ignored" and not "missed." I say this because it soon became apparent that *all* signals are perceived. The human brain is so incredibly capable it misses nothing.

Years ago, when I was asking people to be alert for me, that was the wrong thought. What I needed was for somebody to grab an equivalent of a two-by-four and whack me, and say, "Look, you just got a signal. What are you going to do about it?"

On Side Two of the "signal" card I have the following sub-questions: "Did somebody say something important that I missed?" "Did a piece of machinery try to tell me something?" "Am I protecting my possessions?" "Did something happen today that indicates a change for the worse in my body or mind?"

(Once, when I asked that last, I realized that some time during the day I had started sniffling. I promptly took an anti-cold pill; and the sniffles went away.)

It's a little difficult to know when you've lost some of your marbles. If it doesn't affect your financial situation, then we're not concerned with it here. But if you wonder about it, my suggestion is watch to see if your friends are shaking their heads over you oftener.

How to Respond to a Signal

Finally—a note of caution and a word of advice similar to that which I urged upon individuals who are naturally excessively non-victim types. Meaning that if you already possess an over-sensitivity to small signals, this section is not for you.

How do you determine if the foregoing admonition applies to you?

A true signal simply tells you something:

- A machine makes a wrong sound.
- Your business associate engages in a private deal with some-one without letting you know, and you get wind of it.
- Your boss fails to say hello three successive mornings.
- Etc.

What do these things mean? They may mean nothing, or very little, or a lot.

If they promptly evoke from you an emotional reaction—e.g., anger or suspicion—you're already on the wrong path.

This is particularly true if you have a back history of quarrels with former associates, ruptures of relationships and broken friendships.

What you should do is use your reasoning mind. And either bide your time or have a peaceful confrontation. Get the facts. Be alert. And don't be any more vulnerable than you have to be. Ever. Don't make accusations; ask questions.

Regard the signaler as a game player. Make your own moves as in a game of skill.

I recommend to people who have an extreme sensitivity to small signals the book *Business as a Game* by Albert Z. Carr. And I recommend further that if your automatic reaction to signals has, in fact, been anger or suspicion, and you can afford it, you might try the new bio-feedback idea. In this method you utilize an electroencephalograph as a means of training yourself to produce alpha waves. The purpose would be to stabilize you, to calm those instant antagonistic emotions.

If you are not sensitive to small signals—and that's most of us—then bio-feedback with its alpha wave therapy is probably not for you.

11

Eleventh Quality of the Money Personality: Maintaining Winning Habits

The money personality trains himself in winning habits.

Charles B. Roth, in his encyclopedia *Secrets of Success,* writes:

> A good sales habit . . . is to sit down and construct in your mind a conversation you expect to have with someone whom you have to influence favorably. You try to imagine what he will say, what you will say in reply. You try to think up objections he will raise to your proposal, then work out in your own mind what you will say in rejoinder.

The foregoing is an excellent example of the hundreds of tips provided in Roth's outstanding book, which I ran into only a few weeks ago, and recommend highly.

Mr. C., one of my three wealthy men, always did what I have just detailed, and did it long before the observant Mr. Roth wrote his book. As Mr. C. explained it to me, "You can feel pretty foolish when the person you are talking to brings up a point that you should have thought of, but you didn't; and so you have no answer for it, and that's the end of that transaction, with several precious hours wasted."

What Mr. Roth recommends, and Mr. C. does, is a good success habit to get into.

There are other good habits, probably far more than you will ever need; but let me describe a few of the more important.

Making a Habit of Being Decisive

Behind every sound moneymaking decision is a systematic thought. The problem arises. The person who has to decide yes or no *consults that system* within himself, and then (often to the surprise of other persons present who do not have a system) he renders an immediate verdict for a reason which—if he states it—shows that he has in fact made a penetrating analysis of the matter.

Several questions are involved at the conscious level of such an internalized consultation: (1) Does this proposal have any merit at all? (2) Is it relevant to my business? (3) How does it fit in with the plans that my associates and I worked out at the beginning of the year (which will not be sidetracked except in an emergency situation)? (4) Will it improve my performance in some phase of what I am doing to make money? (5) If I were to set this suggestion in motion, what would it do to or for my moneymaking set-up?

If someone has taken the trouble to make a serious suggestion for improving your money situation, and if the suggestion is not suitable, your rejection of it should be gentle and appreciative.

Say, perhaps, "It doesn't at first sight look as though it will fit into our program, but let me think about it—and thanks all the same."

If you are at the receiving end of such a remark, you should assume that those words mean death for your idea—but you also must appreciate that it's been nicely said.

Poor Decisions Often Have Hidden Reasons

Now I come to a less desirable reason for a decision: a type which the decider should become aware of and watch out for.

In his book *Think and Grow Rich,* Napoleon Hill (what a fabulous name, eh?) says that all of the top rich men that he has ever known were strongly sexed individuals.

We may well imagine that there is some kind of a "normal" drive in this genital department which energizes its possessor and motivates him to even greater efforts.

However, I have observed a less fortunate aspect of the sex drive.

Executives do office morale harm when they date one of the girls or women workers of the firm. Such a woman often makes irrational demands; and so instead of having his full reasoning brain available for his work, the executive spends his time thinking how he can placate her.

Worse, in all his decisions throughout the day when he appears to be asking himself silent, suitable questions about the matter at hand, the truth is he is asking himself if he can fit the business matter into a schedule that will not conflict with his obligations to his secret girl friend—instead of the other way around.

This is why good companies desire stable family situations, which include a wife who is sexually compatible with her husband. They want a family condition where the man is not forced to be out on the prowl because of his wife's sexual hang-ups.

Do not compare the darker picture that I have been detailing with a highly energetic male's occasional one-night stands in which he establishes once more for himself that he is still a man of power. Such "proofs" of masculinity are really unnecessary, but they do occur; and they are what Napoleon Hill was referring to.

Developing "Warding-Off" Thoughts

A friend told me the following:

He and a colleague worked for a very difficult boss. The colleague could not accustom himself to the personality of this superior, J.S., and spent a good portion of his spare time recounting the boss's faults and daily stupidities.

One day my friend asked his disgusted colleague, "How many

spare time hours a month would you estimate that you spend thinking and talking about J.S.?" (the boss).

"Oh—" after a long pause—"thirty hours."

My friend didn't argue with the figure, though he did consider it an underestimate. Instead, he asked his next question: "How much time do you think J.S. thinks and talks about you in a month?"

Longer pause. "About ten minutes," the other man said finally in a subdued tone.

Knowing what I know now, I doubt if that would have stopped this employee's disturbed feelings and resultant need to let off steam.

What a person must have in a stress situation, or after a traumatic experience, is what I have for many years called a "warding-off thought."

How long should you feel grief or shock over a severe loss? I know a widow who still talks abut her husband's death twenty years ago as if it had happened yesterday. As a result she has never been able to make a new life for herself.

In our day when men die five to ten years before their wives, a normal widow goes through a visible cycle—i.e., visible to her friends. For a few months, she has a subdued appearance, and a quiet withdrawn existence. Then one day she goes out and buys herself a new dress and gets her hair done by a hairdresser. The upswing that thus begins includes lots of physical movement, of going places, visiting, shopping.

How do some individuals successfully break free of the thrall of loss, while others—like Widow One—can't?

The one who broke free either created her own warding-off thought, or accepted one from among the many offered to survivors by friends, neighbors, and relatives.

To explain what a warding-off thought is: Some years ago, after I had co-authored *The Hypnotism Handbook* with a psychologist, a friend asked me to determine if hypnotism might be useful for a completely paralyzed woman who lived with her sister in a remote suburb.

I visited the woman several times, trying all available techniques. Finally convinced that nothing could be done to help her out of her situation, and having found out that she was deeply religious, I posted on the ceiling above her a line from the poet, Milton:

> They also serve who only stand and wait.

I asked her sister to leave the words up there for a year, so that the suggestion and philosophy implicit in it could really take effect and comfort her.

That is a warding-off thought.

It's a sort of one-sentence philosophy which the individual brings to mind whenever the old dark thoughts come up—in short whenever he (she) regresses to a time of loss or grief.

Positive thinking? If so, it's very specific. Most people have only one or two that do something for them. All the ones that I have heard are variations of a surprisingly small total of basic ideas.

Widows are often told: "My dear, it's time you started making a new life for yourself"; "You have to think of yourself (and the children)."

A millionaire real estate man told me: "I have one simple rule: Don't look back!" Meaning, don't dwell on the troubles that are behind you.

My own warding-off thoughts are: "No use crying over spilt milk," and "I'm going to snap out of this sooner or later, so why not right now."

When you have finally found an acceptable warding-off thought, a phrase that "fits" you, it starts to work within minutes after you say it aloud.

Here are some more:

- This too shall pass.
- What will all this mean a hundred years from now?
- It (whatever it is that has happened) is not really important.
- I can learn a lesson from what happened.
- Every experience, bad or good, has some value for my future.
- Count your blessings.

- Tomorrow is going to be another wonderful day.
- God works in mysterious ways—and I know that under His guidance this will all work out.
- I shall overcome.

If you are not easily disturbed, then you may already have a perfectly good warding-off philosophy. If you don't know what your thought is, you might look over a difficult past experience from which you recovered, and notice how you did it.

To the colleague of my friend of long ago, I would now suggest the one about "What will all this matter a hundred years from now?" With that as a barrier between him and J.S. he could ride through day after day of a curmudgeon's discourtesy and scarcely notice it.

Really.

The Power of Stick-to-it-iveness

It is interesting that some people are able to persist at a task until it is completed, while others can never seem to finish anything they start.

These latter individuals dally, or become like the shifting sand in the desert.

Naturally, an employee of a company learns while on the job to dispense with impulses that lead him to finish nothing. If he doesn't his services are dispensed with.

We observe him completing tasks which he has been assigned. And there on the job he should notice that most of the work has a beginning, a middle, and—yes—an ending. Tasks are of finite length, and have a specific number of operations. Indeed, on an assembly line the details of a given production are organized with complete precision. The entire operation all the way to the finished product is broken down into a step-by-step procedure.

If you are the type that dallies, a non-finisher, then your first step is to observe that quality in yourself, and under no circumstances go into business on your own. Seek the role of employee for your survival, and remain in that role until you can establish in spare time activity the ability to finish what you start.

How do you begin something like that?

There is an old Chinese proverb which goes: "The journey of a hundred miles begins with one step."

A successful business is organized. The successful executives of that business organize themselves to do their job better. A lower-level employee can do the same—and his ability to do so will under some circumstances commend him to his superiors.

So perhaps you can begin your hundred-mile journey at work in what seems to be the most routine of tasks.

Now that you have read these lines, take out a clean sheet of paper, and write down your duties in the order of their *importance*. Next, list them in the order in which they have to be done. In other words, put down first what absolutely has to come first whether it's important or not.

Thereafter, each day, do the necessary, then the important, and the least essential at the end of the day.

Can't be bothered? Okay, get yourself a Coke or a coffee and read on.

Making a Start

Need extra cash?

Sell a good article from door to door in your spare time. Saturday daytimes is a good time to begin, partly because people don't like nighttime house-to-house salesmen these days.

If what you have to offer doesn't sell fairly regularly, don't bother with that item. Scan the magazines for possibilities. Use your God-given good sense. (We've discussed that before: Quality Five.)

Suppose it sells. Keep going. You're on Step One on the hundred-mile journey to becoming a good salesman. On your next vacation, put in full time on the selling. See what you can do in eight hours.

"B-but what about my vacation?" you whisper weakly. "The family has sort've been planning a trip to the mountains."

Are you kidding? Get back on that selling job. In ten years take them on a trip to the moon, first class. If your vacation-time selling *proves* that you can make a living from house-to-house salesmanship, you might seriously consider quitting your job. If you do, continue house-to-house selling *by yourself* for several months. Does the product actually sell regularly? Yes. Boy, you may really have a good thing here. What's the next step?

Place it in the grocery stores?

Don't be a nut! That's probably the *last* step. That requires production, and advertising, on a vast scale. In a grocery store people buy nationally advertised brands or cut-price articles.

Besides, if you're selling some other person's product you'll have to protect your situation with him before you take *any* steps up. If the product is your own, then you have an even bigger problem: manufacture in quantity and protection of your ownership.

What is gradational scale evolvement of a business for what you have to sell? If it's your own product, or you can get control of it for your area, you have two next-step possibilities: (1) You become a sales manager and hire salesmen to go on the road, or (2) you continue as a loner, but now you divide your calling time. Half as before goes on your bread-and-butter house calls. The second half of your time is spent calling on small businesses that—you have analyzed—may buy your product in dozen lots (instead of the one-sale-at-a-time you make door to door). If your analysis is correct, then each call becomes more lucrative.

In all of this hard work, you're not only earning a living, you're learning.

Incidentally, these days the item you sell should retail for something over $3.00 but not above $7.00, generally. Don't offer a 50-cent product. That's like asking for a handout in our abundant economy.

The step up to utilizing other salesmen has numerous problems. Control of the product—as I've already said. If by some remote chance, you have actually invented the thing yourself, and if it's really good (and you're not kidding an idiot—you), then prepare to do some careful thinking and even more careful doing. Don't show anyone how to make the item, not even your best friend. Retain the secret, even if you have to visit each salesmanager's home regularly and stir in the decisive ingredient. Print on the can: "Patent Applied For."

A patent costs about $5000 before you're through, so it's not necessarily something you can afford right away.

First-step people are too numerous to count in the history of success.

Begin with One Product

"Coco" Chanel, the woman after whom the perfume Chanel #5 is named, started as a couturier in Paris in a little dress shop with *one* dress—meaning, she made many copies of that dress and sold them. To someone who has designed one satisfactory dress, stepping up to two is not really hard. When beautiful "Coco" died in 1971, the Chanel empire was grossing $160 million a year.

Do you have any kind of artistic talent? Can you or your wife make a cute lampshade?

Make it and sell it. Make another one just like it. Sell *it.* Keep going with that single design. Where do you sell such masterpieces? In any large city there are brokers for *everything.* You can either sell through them, or take the product to a small shade shop. Or else try selling it house to house.

One item is your start.

Do you work at an hourly wage in a big plant operating on government contracts? Look around and see if there's anything being made for the contract that has a lot of breakage on it, and actually requires a special skill which is just not available from hourly workers.

In your home on your own equipment, figure out a method for making that item with a minimum breakage. The reason it's possible is that often *no one* has had the time to give good engineering thought to that small aspect of the overall project. There are simply too many things for the engineers to do, entirely apart from figuring out solutions on that level.

You do it. Then set yourself up under the fictitious name of, for example, Utopian Products. Make sure someone else in your city is not already using that name. By looking in the phone book, of course. (Any other fictitious name will do as well.) Various states have different methods whereby you can acquire legal ownership of such a name fairly simply, which you can find out by calling the relevant city department.

That done, put in a bid as a sub-contractor to make that part.

Everywhere you look in our economy you observe people who have the managerial skill to operate a business dealing in many items. By the time you see them, they know so much that you don't that it seems impossible for you ever to duplicate their immense, easy skill. But you can, eventually.

The Full-Time Job of Playing the Stock Market

I once knew fairly well a man who had acquired a rare ability. He made his living exclusively from playing the stock market. He put in a full eight-hour day on his "job" every day that the market was open. Naturally, I was curious about his methods, and was interested to find out what he did during those eight hours.

Part of the time was spent at his work desk, and part at one of the trading offices through which he personally conducted his transactions. A lot of information comes in to a brokerage house each day. Some of it directly or indirectly influenced stocks in his portfolio. He told me that one of his principal advantages over the average good investor was that he had taught himself how to read a company's annual report. Apparently there is certain language in these reports which requires special knowledge to appreciate its meaning.

Thus, if for any *good* reason he became interested in a stock, he would read its annual report as soon as it was published—read it *several times.* It was important to examine such reports quickly, because all over the country other investors as knowledgeable as he were doing the same thing. If the report telegraphed to such experts what they were looking for, they would start to buy at once. And of course then the stock would go up.

My friend spent additional time each day reviewing the information he had on the companies in which he had invested.

Seeing this man through these few comments, we glimpse an expert at work in an exotic occupation. It was he who recommended to me the book, *The Evaluation of Common Stocks,* which is listed elsewhere.

All successful people operate by a method. When such a person awakens in the morning, he does not have a confusion in his mind about the forthcoming day. He knows something worth knowing, finance-wise: real estate, management, running a production line—in which he understands every step, and so on.

Knowing with such certainty makes it possible for him easily to begin something, proceed to its middle, and then finish it. When a person has reached the top of the heap, he has thousands of memories of doing things in his back history. These are like positively charged particles all moving in the same going-forward direction.

He is the man who has not only taken the first step on that hundred-mile journey to success, but has also personally walked the entire distance and knows the terrain. To get there, he had to climb many a hill and cross many a swift river. The lessons, and the knowing energy of the miles and the years, are now in his brain.

And the vast sums of money he made are in his bank account.

Advice on Playing the Stock Market

1. You must be prepared to give it some time and thought.

2. Do *not* simply buy a stock and put it away, while it goes up and down, up and down—up above what you paid for it, and down below. Your job when in the market is to make money when it goes up, and also to make money when it does down.

3. In order to make money when a stock is going down, you sell it *short.* This requires you to have about 60% of the value of the stock on deposit with the brokerage firm.

4. When you are actively in the market, after you have bought a stock *and* it goes up (but you're holding it for further rise), put a Stop-Loss on it above what you paid for it, and put a reasonable Sell order in at the price you would like to get for it. Most active

operators also put a Stop-Loss below what they paid for it. The reason for this is to cut losses to a minimum, and they don't want to be bothered with a stock that doesn't do what it is supposed to.

5. There is of course a wealth of information available on stocks, ranging all the way from computerized tapes through numerous market letters to a number of interesting systems, each based on a shrewd analysis of a significant aspect of the market. There are even phone numbers (frequently changed) that you can dial and from which you can receive daily recorded advice.

6. If you made gains (profits) during any year, the time to take your losses is at year-end. Reason: You balance losses off against gains for tax purposes. You may re-buy the stock, but you must wait a while before doing so.

Using Elegant Language

Although I personally find scant occasion to use the four-letter words, nor have I ever been to a Nudist camp, I feel there is nothing basically wrong with *any* word, nor with the act of exposing the human body in its natural state for good-health reasons.

Advocates of naturalism have much that is rational to say for their point of view, though, alas, many of them are poor advocates. They have rage attitudes. They are visibly alienated from society and are not being natural for the sake of sanity.

Everything has its place and its time.

If someone pointedly starts to tell me about the functions of his digestive tract at a dinner table, I usually find it distasteful and out of place. Very little shocks me these days, but when my little gray cells tell me that somebody is directing vulgarity or shock *intent* at me, he may well lose me right there as a potential friend or ally.

I was once present when a man made a vulgar remark to a rather good-looking woman. She said in instant reply, "You sonofabitch, don't you ever open your dirty mouth to me again!"

Which was a little startling. But it was the first and the last time I ever heard her say anything in inelegant language.

There is a possibility that the four-letter word has its place where you have to convince primitive types that you are a Real Man. This particular masculine need is actually ridiculous in our day in America. But often you don't have the opportunity to deliver a lecture to this effect to people who seem to require that such language be used in their presence.

Generally, the four-letter vocabulary seems to have its best usage in a military barracks and among teen-agers. In the barracks, cursing and four-letter language serve as a release of tension and a bracing against fear. Teens appear to gain, from the extensive use of inelegant language, the feeling of being grown-up.

A few years ago, I had occasion to give talks to about fifty service clubs in my area. I don't recall during that entire experience hearing a single four-letter word spoken by any of the two thousand or so businessmen whom I had the honor to address.

I would say that that is the significant factor to notice. These are essentially educated people. They read good books. They keep up with knowledge. They speak courteously to each other and to their customers.

My suggestion: Read poetry in your off hours, and speak the great and beautiful English language with poetic skill, in a cultivated, resonant voice if you are a man, and in a sweet or lilting voice if you are a woman.

Staking Out a Stake

Conrad Hilton arrived in a Texas oil town in 1919 with $5011 in good American currency pinned inside his shirt. With this stake, which in his autobiography, *Be My Guest,* he clearly considers a nominal sum, he started the great Hilton hotel chain.

In a sense it was nominal. But in 1919 it could buy $16 to $17 thousand in 1970s value. In those years, my father earned about $1500 a year as a small town attorney. Getting hold of $5000 free and unspoken for (i.e., uncommitted) was impossible for, I would guess, 98% of the entire adult male population of the American continent. And I wouldn't be surprised if that weren't also true of 95% or more today.

So if by any chance you have an uncommitted $5000—i.e., you

don't need it for living expenses, and it isn't a loan that you have to pay back—then you are in a pretty good situation.

What to do with it?

When I was in Kansas on the occasion on which I saw the St. Louis Browns, I was sitting one day in the office of a Wichita oil and real estate millionaire. The phone rang. Long distance from Dallas, Texas. The conversation was brief. My host said, $6000." I saw him write the figure on his calendar and make a note to himself beside it. Then he said, "When?" A moment later he said, "All right."

After he hung up, he said to me, "That was a broker in Texas. He needed $6000 each from several persons for a deal. I've let him have money before, and I've always got it back with a large increase."

Unfortunately, I didn't ask him how much more, but if you will recall the people who advanced Henry Ford his stake, they got back thousands-fold.

If you have $5000, you need to find one or more persons like that broker. What this means is that the person you look for has a past record of successful deals, and is already well-to-do from these previous ventures, but needs cash constantly for new projects.

Unfortunately, the average person has no idea how to locate such people. What usually happens is that the owner of $5000 is approached by a man who has a project in mind and who needs money for it. This man has no clear record of past success, but he is anxious to be rich. A small percentage of such men may actually be capable of becoming wealthy.

To find this small percentage, you apply the rules of this book. How many—and *which*—of the qualities does he have? He absolutely must be a non-victim and be able to charge a profit. He must be able to make his project real. And he must not be the type of person who as soon as he acquires money is off concupiscenting. His project should be well reasoned out; but naturally *you* should be able to determine its validity on the basis of your own good reasoning and *your* possession of the qualities I have described here—if you intend to put in a good portion of that $5000.

Generally speaking, you do *not* give a man without a previous success record more than a small contribution to his needed sum. If you have confidence in him, point out that his hope has to be a syndicate-type operation. Give him $500, and not $5000. A man who cannot raise money among his friends and acquaintances lacks the ability to make things real and has never been a gift giver.

A good invention is still one of the best things to invest in. When it pays off, the sky is often the limit on the profits.

Having pointed a direction—two directions, in fact—let me hastily once more make crystal clear that this is *not* a book designed to tell you how or where to make a million. Its purpose is to show you what kind of person you have to be before you involve yourself *or your stake* in any project.

Conrad Hilton operated throughout his career like that Texas broker. If he saw a good possibility, he called upon wealthy business acquaintances and received sums of up to a million from each of them. It is very likely that finding people like that to associate with, and building credit and goodwill with them, should be one of *any* money seeker's continuing purposes.

Habits of the Winner—and the Loser

The Winner's	*The Loser's*
Daily exercise	Boasting
Being on time	Dwelling on the past
Keeping a promise	Repeating oneself
Social graces	Social disgraces
Truthfulness and integrity	Carelessness and lying
Courtesy	Disregard of others
Cheerfulness	Quick anger
Specific-ness	Sitting in judgment on the world
Elegant language	Vulgarity

12

Twelfth Quality of the Money Personality: Escaping Orientation to Failure

The money personality orients to money or to a winner.

Quality Twelve is a product of my telling a group of people some of my ideas about the money personality.

One of the group, a man, did virtually an instant analysis of his own situation. Then he said in an astonished voice, "Do you know that I have in my home a person who has just about all of the qualities you've described—only whenever she tries to do something about it, I squelch her with the statement that we can't afford it."

The "person" with "just about all those qualities" was his wife.

She had, as he described her, good taste in just about everything, and a strong desire to own things. She schemed constantly to bypass his resistance, and had managed in 15 years to sneak into the house some antique furniture and antique jewelry, but she did for the most part defer to his dictum about being unable to afford luxuries.

Except for her few purchases, everything they owned was junk. And they had always lived in rented apartments or houses.

As of this writing—less than six years later—they own an $18,-000 equity in a $50,000 home, $25,000 worth of antique furniture (which keeps increasing in value), and some shrewdly bought land worth nearly a hundred thousand dollars.

The shrewd person who achieved all this was the wife. And it all began when the husband had that super-speed insight and removed his squelching hand from her beautiful natural abilities.

What do we need to observe here? What is Quality Twelve as revealed to me by this man's reaction to hearing what you have been reading about the money personality?

Answer: The thing that I noticed has essentially nothing to do with him. I was startled by *her.* From the beginning she had those numerous money personality qualities. And yet she had allowed one man—her husband—to stop her from using them.

Could it be that there was something in the human psyche that could, of itself, cancel out eleven "go" qualities?

I started analyzing the problem by thinking in terms of the dependency that some people feel on others. This is a widely observed condition in women, and usually derives from their early brainwashing by the culture.

"Dependency" is not exactly what I finally came up with, but it is a related phenomenon. So a small discussion of it is a good lead-in to an understanding of Quality Twelve.

Orientation Toward Dependency

Through an unnoticed dependency, a man (or woman) can indeed lose all that he has gained through possession of the other eleven qualities. I know a situation where a man gradually signed the stock of his factory over to his mistress. When he died, his wife and children got nothing.

Although dependency is a broad spectrum, often involving things as well as people, I have found that most individuals understand the concept best when it is restricted to dependency on people. The persons I have the hardest time with are, first, the so-called rugged individualist, who believes that he is free of all that kind of nonsense; second, the poor devil whose need for self-esteem has no visible ceiling; and, third, the fellow who thinks that all problems are physical.

Number One feels that his philosophy of power saved him from that particular aberration. We need only make one observation about him: Is he rich? If he is, then his dependency can remain hidden. Whatever it is, it's good for him. But if he is a rugged individualist and has no money, he'd better take a second look.

Number Two, the conceited one, if he has wealth is likewise no concern of ours. The people like his wife who have to live with him are probably long-suffering and scarcely even notice their continuing anguish and degradation as the guy's conceit impinges on them. But if he's poor, reason with him by pointing out that while no doubt he himself is a very worthy individual (probably full of high ideals), this isn't buying any groceries. If reason doesn't move him, and he won't agree to the solution suggested at the end of this section, then his wife is going to have to go to work, as outlined elsewhere—unless *she* can break *her* emotional dependency feelings in relation to him.

Number Three usually attributes any failures he has had to the fact that he fell ill, and while ill his business collapsed. Each person I talked to who had had this happen, tried to make out that his situation was a genuine one. My thesis is that the person becomes ill as he faces failure. For some reason, usually because of actions taken in connection with a dependency madness, he begins to fail—and then he falls ill. The failure is then finalized.

Since almost everybody agrees that this is what happens to those other people, but they were the exception—with *them* it was *really* the illness—let me simply say that there are no exceptions.

What Your Philosophy May Reveal

The condition of dependency can be extreme and yet not be visible, except in a philosophy. An example would be the person who places peace of mind above everything else. Such an individual is looking back to the early age of dependency when he had no worries and all his needs were supplied by his mother and father, who asked nothing in return from him. This can originally have been a very short period of time—a single idyllic summer, which ever afterwards is correlated at some level of being with peace, comfort, security, and the way things should really be.

And then there are individuals who wait to receive prosperity as a gift rather than as a result of their mastery of the environment. They still dream of the kind of magical solutions that were possible in the childhood dependence period.

Then a glittering new bicycle, or a golden-haired doll, would appear one day and would be presented with loving pleasure by parents or grandparents.

Magic, yes. But the magic of childhood dependence.

According to psychologists, most marital love begins when you meet someone who at some deep of the mind is identified with (A), that parent of the opposite sex, whom you either wanted and couldn't have, or (B), the parent or other doting adult who gave you that idyllic summer or that gift.

So if you are a woman, the only thing you can ever blame your husband for is that he is not really a grandfather-substitute; and if you are a man, you can blame your wife for not being like mother.

Your Hidden Security Need

Regardless of which of these constituted your background, as you grow up you keep looking for a place, a location, in relation to some person or group, where the part of it that made the biggest impression on you can all happen again. Or, where it can happen in a reverse way to satisfy the scarcity (false need) that was built up.

When you find such a location, you move in on it, and you will not budge from it of your own free will. You will have to be carried, ill or screaming, to that kind of trash can into which clinging people are sometimes (though not often) discarded.

What does happiness mean to you? Whether you know it or not, the low-grade happiness of people in our present era is the result of their forcing themselves into such a location and staying there no matter what thunderbolts fall around them, or how much the person—if an individual is involved (usually a husband, wife, parent, or child)—struggles to get away.

Am I writing in riddles?

I'll try to explain.

Because of a childhood dependence, or need, everybody is—and here is the word—*oriented* to something or someone.

I call this a location, because you have to be in the vicinity of, or in orbit around, and at some near distance to the person, or group, involved.

Such a dependency limits your identity, restricts your ability to adapt or change, holds you forever waiting or forever accepting the sub-optimum. It's as though they poured the concrete while you were standing in it, and it hardened before you even noticed that you were caught. Now you think that's the way life is, and you've got yourself a whole set of rationalizations to explain to other people why you're there.

If the kind of dependency I'm talking about is your principal problem in non-money making, then you've got to step out of that concrete.

How—if it's as solidly set as I have described?

Stepping Out of the Orientation Glue

There is a wonderful story in science illustrating the mechanical principle that if you had a long enough crowbar properly braced on a fulcrum, you could move our planet out of its orbit with your little finger.

What kind of "crowbar of the mind" do we have to devise to get you out of the non-moneymaking dependency "habit" you are in and into a money-success habit?

Well, the "crowbar" is waiting for your finger to push it. That is, it's waiting for about 80 percent of individuals to some greater or lesser degree.

Pushing it may not turn out as well for you as it did for the man described at the beginning of this chapter. Recall—all he did was cease suppressing a natural winner. That—it should be made clear—is not the best solution for anyone. The best solution is that he acquire *all* of the twelve qualities, personally.

But it is a good interim thing to do while the necessary time passes for you to do that acquiring.

Right now let's take a close look at what you should notice about yourself and the people around you in connection with Quality Twelve.

Using a Magical Crowbar Against Failure

The natural money personality can be recognized by his past money deeds.

A couple belonged to that large group of intermediate intellectual types in which the man's training is technical. He had reached the point where his gross income was about $15,000 a year. Numerous millions of people make that in this country, and still have no money because after tax and other deductions are taken off, the gross has come down to a sad-looking net. Buying a new suit for the man was a major, unwelcome expense in this family. The wife found the way to success. *How did she do it?*

Let me summarize the sequence of actions that led to their greater affluence. To find bargains, you have to beat the bushes. This woman did. It was a time when it was hard to sell real estate, and correspondingly easy to buy it. And so she went around inspecting houses and waiting for the bargain that had to be available on such a buyer's market. She found it. The owner was a man who had taken on too much property. He said, in effect, "Lady, I owe two years' back taxes and a year's payments." He was desperate. If the loan company foreclosed, then they could sue him for what was due and he'd lose both house and money. Actually, the loan company people had already had too many properties come back on them, and so they were glad to let her take over the payments.

She borrowed what was needed to pay off the indebtedness from a brother and a friend, whereupon the family left their rented house, and moved into this beautiful home. Monthly payments were about the same as their rent had been, only now most of it was interest and taxes, all tax deductible.

Her husband, unthinkingly relieved—and feeling that the millennium was already here—looked forward to a more leisurely existence: more books, a better vacation, and so on. "Oh, no, we don't," said his wife. "What we saved on that $250-plus that we no longer pay taxes on, now goes into getting hold of assets."

More antiques, in this instance. On her house-hunting forays, she'd also happily dropped in on antique stores; to catch the bargains you really have to see what comes in from day to day. She had about $60 a month to play with, so she was soon making small weekly payments on a variety of treasures. The beautiful home began to shine inside as well as outside.

A couple of garage sales disposed of unwanted utility stuff and brought a little more cash. But the big item, the land, required a more decisive event—and provides us with the clue for recognizing the magical "crowbar" in your house.

A few years earlier the wife's mother had died and had left her about $5,000. The husband managed to siphon $3,000 off into various necessities: car repair, then a down payment on another car, etc.—badly thought-out expenditures, for the most part. (It should have been either a car *or* car repair, but not both, for example.)

But the wife had put the balance of $2,000 into government bonds. And there, tearfully, she made her stand. Her somewhat emotional resistance to encroachment on those bonds was based on her feeling that her mother's estate should *not* be dribbled away.

And so, when the opportunity came, she had $2,000 to put down on several acres of land—total cost $18,000 plus 6½% interest.

"If we lose it," she said, "okay. But it will have been a good try."

The prospect of losing a major asset finally alerted the easygoing but hardworking type she had married. For him, it was like receiving an assignment; and that he could do.

What happened: On the edge of her acreage a small city was built *in toto* by an insurance company. The property zoomed in value, and she had a number of immediate offers for it, beginning at $40,000—all of which she turned down.

Was this luck? No. First of all what happened proved once again the old argument of real estate firms that one good investment is often worth more than a lifetime of hard work.

Provided—let me add—that the investment is made by a winner.

The main point I want to make here is that every potential "crowbar" *has something like that $2000 in bonds in his or her background.*

And *that* is how you can recognize if there is one in your household.

Overcoming Problems Of Victim Marriages

Another typical example (to show you the variations on the theme): A young couple got married. Though he had consistently earned more money than his bride, it developed that at the time of the wedding he owed $3,800 and she had about $3,000 in her savings account. Discovering his financial plight was a great disappointment to her. She had thought of her money as the down payment on a small house. But she braced herself, and paid off most of the debt.

That young woman's possession of that $3,000 is evidence that she's a "crowbar" type.

Now, here's a male example (for smart young marriage-minded women to observe): This girl met a transport worker, originally from Texas. His dream was to own a ranch of his own, in other words he already had an assignment in his head, a direction. More important, at the time she met him he had several cows on some land he was buying in northern California. She considered these good indicators, and she married him ten years ago. She was right. They now own a ranch of many hundreds of acres and many, many more heads of cattle (though it really doesn't take many cows in today's market to make a living).

Remember, if all this had only been talk, it would not have been enough. Talk has an assignment aspect, yes; but a dream that is still merely in words is not it. Something must already have been earned, or actually accomplished.

The exception to the foregoing would be a man who is *well on the way* to getting a valid university degree that points to a profession. *His* plans can be meaningful.

Here is a second male example, to make sure you get the picture. A young woman asked me at one of my talks if I would advise her to marry a man who had a business in junk metal. The idea of an attractive girl wed to a junk man stopped me for a moment. I had old images in my head that I had to dispose of, of the ragged types of my childhood who did this kind of business.

After a few questions, I quickly brought myself up to the present-age, old-metal condition. And—it turned out—correctly pictured a modern young man with expert sales ability and a lot of physical energy devoted to collecting something that was very much in demand these days.

The questions I asked her, and her answers, were: "How long has he been doing this?" "Over five years." "Then he's over the hump, if ever there was one?" "Oh, yes." "What kind of car does he drive?" "A Ford Galaxie." "What year?" (It was the previous year model.) "Does he live in an apartment?" "He owns a small house," she replied. "Marry him," I said.

Please note: Merely owning a late-model car is not sufficient indication. Wastrels, who will never amount to anything financially (until they read this book and acquire the twelve qualities), drive some of the fanciest cars on the streets. Here is the question to ask yourself in connection with a car: Is he driving a machine that fits his income and work?

What to Do About a Non-Crowbar

Final thought on good indications: If a male drives an old jalopy at 18, okay; at 25 something is wrong.

Anyway, look for something like those examples. They're all the evidence you need. If you look, and can't make sense out of the behavior you're looking at, you need a special dose of Quality Five: discover through a game what's wrong with your reasoning. If you see the problem, and cannot bring yourself to act on it, then most likely you suffer from orientation sickness: Quality Twelve.

Okay—what do you do?

I have said that in my estimation 80% of men are victims, and 80% of women non-victims. (This is a rough estimate.) By simple arithmetic, we may therefore calculate that the majority of non-victim women are married to victim men.

If a woman could do it, a limited solution to this problem could be for the woman to throw the sucker out on his ear and find herself a man who is not a victim. But that's not a practicable mass solution. The anxious-to-remarry non-victim woman would find herself searching for a non-victim husband in a world where 80% of the men are victims.

There are not enough non-victim males to go around. So the solution has to be worked out for the majority, probably including you, without dramatic changes in your private life.

Within this in-motion frame, essentially two solutions are possible. This is because victim males divide broadly into two, and only two, classifications: those who can be reasoned with by a woman, and those who cannot.

First, notice—and get his agreement—that your husband is a victim-type male.

If your husband agrees that he is a victim (and he really is), then he is a man who can be reasoned with, and you, his wife, should forthwith become the family business manager—provided you meet the requirements already described.

(In deciding if a man is a victim type, let's put aside right now the need of so many women to make a perfect husband out of the peculiar fellow they married.)

Get this can-be-reasoned-with husband to agree that in any discussion involving property, or money, you will talk to buyer, or seller, alone. He may later be useful in reading contracts and pointing out to you pitfalls in it. But he must agree not to walk in on you and agree to everything the buyer or seller wants.

What this means, madam, is that your husband is no longer allowed to take the car in to have it repaired; you do that, and you talk to the repair man. If inadvertently a swindle has taken place in spite of all your precautions, don't say to your husband, "Now, you phone that man, or you go to see him and straighten this out like a real man should." That's not it. *You* phone the swindler, or *you* confront in person, and straighten the matter out. Keep remembering that a victim cannot confront a victimizer. Not just *won't* confront him. *Can't.* This is why he mustn't be allowed in the vicinity of any kind of financial transaction involving property, except as a before or after consultant. He may be very wise and knowledgeable, and be able to fill you in on all kinds of facts about cars, contracts, and life. He may have the information—but he cannot use it in an eyeball to eyeball confrontation.

And the reason he mustn't be present at a meeting is that you are vulnerable to him on the level of orientation.

The moment a victim-husband walks in on such a situation, the woman who is oriented to him will find herself seething inwardly but absolutely forced by her orientation to defer to her victim-husband.

The foregoing needs one qualification: Since all women are not financially capable, an additional preliminary to your taking over is that your husband agrees that, in fact, you do have a suitable quantity of Qualities One, Two, and Three through Eleven. (I've given the principal clue.)

An Alternative Solution

Let us suppose, on the other hand, you are married to a man who cannot be reasoned with. What is most often involved, when this happens, is that masculinity is a big thing with him.

If such a subjective husband is a real victim, or failure-oriented (the proof: he hasn't any money, or is losing what he had or inherited), then you have to take a much more practical and severe action.

My advice is to learn a skill, craft, or job that will in later years provide you with a reasonable survival income. I mean, merely learn now; don't go to work now. But—I urge you—don't wait till you have to learn. Learning a job is a good idea anyway. Since males these days die from five to ten years sooner than females, a woman stands a good chance of facing this problem no matter what.

A woman married to a subjective male has what might be called an unstable orientation.

If you are such a woman, and your feeling is that you'd rather be happy than have money, then be sure you're happy. Don't end up with neither money nor happiness.

The moment a woman has established with a victim-husband —and it's a binding deal—that she will be the business head, she has put her little finger on that crowbar and pushed.

What is possible for this couple financially will now happen.

Meanwhile, if the man works at becoming a non-victim, finds a reason for being able to charge more for his services, learns to reason his way to where the money is, and can start making corner lots, etc., real —then in due course of time he can be trusted to have a pen in his hand in the presence of a salesman.

Don't ever assume that this will happen quickly.

How can you know when it has happened?

Dealing with a Severe Orientation Problem

The day you really *feel* that your husband can be trusted with the business affairs of the family—that's it.

If your feeling turns out to be at the delusion level of knowing, then you're in trouble in other ways, and you need to re-examine the whole situation on a non-trust level. An example: There are men so far gone that when given money (by a working wife) to pay the gas bill, they spend it on liquor or other waste.

If you have such a man, and you give him money a second time to pay the gas bill—and he blows it again—lady, you're in orientation trouble so bad that the other eleven qualities are not relevant for your future until you harden your heart and refuse to do such things again.

Don't nag a man like this after the first few hundred times. Either decide to stay with him as he is—or leave him. Statistically, there are no other alternatives.

Coming up to a more normal situation, where trust can exist on simple survival matters, but where the man is a victim-type, a man needs to be protected from a wife who has certain unfortunate spending habits, yet who has actually got a good business head a la Qualities One to Three.

For this special woman, a final cautioning word: Before opening a charge account at a department store, be sure to get your husband's permission. That's not part of your business relation with him.

And, of course, there are those 20% of women who are victims. What if a victim is married to a victim.

Read this book, and help each other.

Got it?

RULE FOR ACHIEVING QUALITY TWELVE

(1)   Orient to a winner—optimum.

(2)   If the person in the family who earns the income is a loser, turn the family budget over to the family non-victim —usually this is the wife. Or, second best, at least turn over the investment budget.

How to Figure Out Your Orientation

It is not always easy to figure out a person's orientation.

One man, Dan, to whom I talked, said, "Look, I'm only a carpenter. I spend my days sawing and hammering, and at the end of the day I'm too beat to do anything but watch television and go to bed early so's I can get up early the next morning. What's my orientation?"

We may observe at once that all Dan's mental images are of wood, tools, and the building trades. My advice to Dan: The abstraction you're making real for your boss (carpentering) is ideal for moneymaking. We don't even need to look for your orientation. Work towards developing the first eleven qualities, and meanwhile buy the book, *How I Turned a Thousand into a Million in Real Estate in My Spare Time.* After you've read it, never again live in a house that you aren't fixing up for future resale at a profit.

Another man, Walter, came up to me at one of my lectures on the twelve qualities and said, "I'm an executive engineer. Because of my responsibilities at the plant, I take my work home with me nights. True, I have a good income, but maintaining my home—which I'm buying—and sending my four children through school and college will continue to eat up my income for another ten years. How can I find what my orientation is and make use of your success qualities to better my finances?"

To Walter I said: "Congratulations on the high position you have already attained. Keep engineering as your way to make a living and do not change your family and home plans. Purchasing a home is a saving method, and ten years is not forever. However, you look like a man who may only need to sharpen his awareness of each of the twelve qualities. I urge this sharpening because any improvement in the first eleven qualities, even if you never find twelve, could bring about a qualitative change. Such a qualitative change will raise you at once to a new height—from which everything will look different. Good luck."

A third person, Renetta—a woman in her fifties—said, "I'm divorced, and have now worked for ten years as a buyer in a department store. Being frugal, I've saved about $20,000 from my divorce settlement and salary, and I am buying my home. I feel unwilling to use my cash to make anything real in my spare time. Right now, I have this money invested in two mutual funds and three real estate investment funds which were recommended to me. I would like to be married for companionship. What's my orientation?"

I told Renetta that she sounded like a financially wise woman, but that there were too many personal aspects in what she had told me for me to determine what her real orientation was, or is. Even prolonged psychological treatment often fails to bring out the facts of why a marriage has broken up. Did Renetta marry a father-substitute? It would take a close inquiry to determine that, and she is no help because now that the marriage is over, she cannot imagine what she ever saw in the man. In short, the evidence has disappeared.

Since there is nothing basically wrong in a woman wanting to be married, her desire to find a companion to share her declining years may not be a clue. But it could be that she is looking for the orientation-substitute. If that is so, then she should take a hard look indeed at the back history of any man who attracts her. If he's divorced, find out—not only from him—what happened. Don't accept too readily the idea that some other woman let go of a real treasure. If he is now successful, maybe after the divorce he had to go out and work—which he always *could* do, but just *wouldn't.* And he'd love to *not,* again. Find out how many times he has changed jobs, and how often he has been employed, and what is the stability of the business location from which he operates.

(I know a man who operates a $300-a-week drapery cleaning service for hotels from his bedroom. He's out of business the moment he stops phoning or gets sick. He is a gay Lothario. In 20 years he has not saved a penny. Don't marry such a man, ladies.)

My fourth and final example, Bob, said, "I'm a clerk, as my father was before me. I'm married, with three children. I pay $178 a month rent out of a take-home pay of $482. I drive a used car, and live up to my income each year. What's my orientation, and is it a factor in my continuing poverty?"

From Bob's account, we can see at once that he seems to be re-living his father's life. There's the orientation. So, for Bob, it is vital that he raise his little finger and push the "crowbar of the mind" as described earlier.

But let's see, specifically, what we can do for Bob with his $482 a month, with a wife and three children. It looks impossible, doesn't it? Can Bob save 10%—let alone 23%—of his income? He says not. He says he can't even buy himself a new suit when he needs it.

Let's slide over one barrier. Let's forget about down payments, and let's forget about chiseling project housing contractors, and let's asume that instead of paying $178 a month rent, Bob is paying that much down each month on the purchase of a house.

Break that down to $30 a month on the principal, and $148 interest. Suddenly, we observe a new plateau. The $30 is a straight monthly saving, for he's building an equity. And the $148, since it is interest, he can deduct from his income tax gross. Suddenly, he is saving $30 plus $29.60 (20% of the interest), a total of $59.60, or over 12% of his take-home pay. At the time of filing his final income tax report, Bob may well discover that the 12% plus his Social Security deductions may together come within a few millimeters of the 23% which I consider a must.

All this without a single extra penny being paid out of Bob's pay check.

Still more, and worse, to come on orientation. But, also, some more solutions.

Overcoming Problems of Victim Partnerships

The money personality operates on the advice of his own lawyer, and trusts the voting power of his own family.

Example One: An inventor, who had been a partner with another individual in a thriving, growing business (based on his inventions), allowed his partner to persuade him to form a corporation consisting of the inventor, the partner, and the partner's son.

Within an hour after the incorporation was legal, the partner and his son called a board meeting. The motion was made by the son to discharge the inventor from his employment with the firm. The motion was carried by a vote of two to one. Next, the motion was made to pay all future profits to the father and son in the form of salary. The motion also carried two to one.

Example Two: A man who was largely responsible for the development of an electronic firm—he was the technical expert—allowed a corporation to be formed with himself, his partner and the partner's wife. Whereupon they ganged up on him two to one, and discharged him from his job, disposing of the profits in fashion similar to Example One.

These two men, being highly capable individuals, both landed on their feet, so to say. They subsequently did well financially, though there have periodically been problems where they again "trusted" somebody unwisely.

Please note that I have placed the word "trusted" in quotes. It needs to be defined.

In each of the foregoing instances of brazen victimization we're looking technically not at a victim but at a person with a Quality Twelve problem.

Both injured parties had been responsible for the initial growth of their respective companies, but each had loyally argued to himself that the partner had made an equal contribution. Both men had a touch of genius in their make-up. Generously, they pretended that they were no better than the partner. This generous impulse prevented them from realizing that in a society where all men are born equal (you've probably heard the joke) some are more equal than others.

In such a situation, the recipient of the generosity—the partner—has to pretend to *himself* something far more irrational: that he is really the better man, because he understands the hard realities of the business world.

By becoming a ruthless businessman—that is, a victimizer—he transcends the genius of his former friend. Thus, he makes himself superior. By a twisted act, he recovers from the shock to his wounded ego of being treated as an equal by a naturally more talented person.

What I have described in these examples involves essentially three qualities. Quality Twelve—orientation—turned men who were normally non-victims into victims (Quality One), and simultaneously the orientation aspect made semi-idiots out of them on Quality Five—good reasoning.

False Victimizer Philosophies

With these examples before us we can also re-evaluate the word "trust." As it has been used historically, it is clearly an underdefined word. By defining it as I have we can see that what it encompasses is a complex psychological problem which required of the naturally more creative and capable man that he pretend to be no better than his non-creative partner; and the partner had the equally complex emotional mental struggle whereby he saved his pride by justifying a criminal act as something that smart people had to do in this cruel world.

All the victimizers that I talked to justified their behavior to themselves with a philosophy of survival, whereby you do what you have to do. The victimizer is convinced that all the "big boys" got their wealth by swindling.

This is untrue. The business world is composed largely of a majority of people who operate with total integrity. Top management consists of individuals who have to justify their acts not only to a board of directors, but also to the banks with which the company deals. Sharp tactics, contrary to public opinion, are frowned on. And any proof of lack of integrity is death.

Most confusion about such matters is attributable to two reasons. On the overt side, there is a small percentage of victimizing (self-justified) types who do engage in shady practices. More subtly, we have the unawareness of the vast mass of essentially negative people who cannot grasp the fact that high-level physical and mental energy make the world go. Until described in this book, such energy has been beyond the reach of the average man.

In addition, the over-all world condition has included a propagandistic attack on Capitalism itself. This propaganda makes the issue that the profit system is basically wrong. Thus, by implication, it tries to make wrong every person who operates a profit-making business.

This is a totally irrelevant argument—first of all because at present no other system has actually accomplished as much as Capitalism. And second because men everywhere live and act within the frame of the system under which they live.

We have not seen the final consequences of the Communist propaganda in this area, but we may safely leave the outcome to our able descendants.

And observe meanwhile that the vast majority of persons who operate on the basis of our profit system are sincere, honest and dependable year after year.

Advice for Orientation Victims

But now in conclusion, what should these two men have done who were voted out of all financial benefit from the corporations in which they continued to own one-third share?

First of all, Quality Five should have told the first man—the inventor—that the best small corporate set-up was to equalize the presence of the other man's son by bringing in a member of his own family.

The second man was unmarried; he should have rejected incorporation, or else had inserted as a part of the corporate agreement that the two original partners would always share equally in the financial returns, which would never be less than that of any other person in the corporation.

I advise both individuals to hold on to their one-third share. If either of the other original board member dies, the victim may be able to challenge any new attempt to deprive him of his share.

One final thought: If you go into business with your lawyer, hire another lawyer to represent you.

Deciding to Escape a Mistaken Orientation

There is a saying that time solves all problems. Time is often very slow about it, and somebody lives that slow time second by minute.

A friend told me of his White Russian father, K., who had been an important government administrator in the Czarist regime, and wealthy in his own right.

Deprived by the revolution of all he owned, he opened a used bookstore in a European city. There was a tiny cot in a rear room of the store, and it was here that K. could be found at almost all hours of the day or evening, stretched out, sound asleep. One day in 1956, some 39 years after the October, 1917, overthrow of Czarism, K. was found on that cot one evening by a customer, dead.

It was believed by his family that the old gentleman had slept away his life because wakefulness confronted him with his demotion from the high position to which by birth and rank he felt himself entitled.

There is a great deal of truth in his family's analysis. But I call the ailment from which K. suffered *orientation*. K. as a child and youth, and in early manhood, was oriented to the belief that a small, elite group of people could own an entire country and its good things; during 38 disillusioning years he could never let go of that orientation.

Under the circumstances the bookstore was actually a very good business for him to be in. He was an educated man, and he had been a reader. So book dealing was within the range of his experience.

If you find yourself shaking your head over K., don't forget that you also are oriented to something. If it is something to do with money, then you have money—there is no other criterion. If your orientation is not to money, or a moneyed person, then you may not in fact have been any smarter than K., orientation-wise.

Undoubtedly, K. had books stolen while he slept. But book buyers would make out their own bills, listing the books they were taking, and slip the bill and the money into the sleeper's pocket. If someone had books to sell, a regular customer would usually awaken K. so that he could take care of the transaction.

In this way, human kindness and good will helped one man to survive a too-rigid orientation to a vanished society.

But orientation on money, or no-money, doesn't have to be forever, as it was with K.

What should you write on a card for Quality Twelve?

List of Possible Orientations

Orientation can be to innumerable things; far too many to list under all their sub-headings. Fortunately, as with the reasons for charging a profit, these multitudinous items are classifiable under a few headings:

- A profession (usually the result of pre-training).
- An occupation (usually the outcome of experience).
- A person (usually a mother or father substitute).
- A group (like the army, or an immigrant community, or the vanished elite society K. was oriented to).
- A philosophy (or ideal, or religion).
- A location, and what goes with it (like that man from Texas. He had images of owning a ranch with cattle. Though he had moved to California, he remained oriented to Texas and what they do on the land in that great cattle state.)
- Money.

Your Orientation Therapy

If you are now oriented to one of the foregoing, and it is proving, or has proved, to be a money orientation—then leave it alone. If on the other hand, your orientation is non-money—so far as you can make out—decide which is most likely your classification; what you write on the card is a question:

"Do I want to continue to be oriented to my _____ ?
(Classification)

By examining this question and its meaning at least once a day, you will presently move yourself off the dime that is associated with your orientation, and onto the dollar (or much more) of a money orientation.

If your orientation is a father or mother substitute, don't feel guilty about wanting to break the orientation. You may discover that the real individual you married has been handicapped by your stereotyped attempt to slap him (her) into a mold emotionally desired by you in order to recreate some childhood security feelings or need.

You might even find that the real person is a far more interesting person than any father or mother variation.

And capable of making more money.

13

Your Own Money Personality

So there you have it. And just to make sure that you do indeed have it, let me spell it out once more:

Your Twelve Qualities

1. In all commercial transactions, the money personality refuses to be a victim, requiring valid agreements in writing, and fulfillment of contracts.

2. The money personality sets himself, or accepts from others, assignments that are specific and that he knows he can carry out.

3. The money personality always has a personal, special reason for charging a profit.

4. The money personality stays awake and alert all day long, preferably with suitable exercise.

5. The money personality understands human nature sufficiently so that he invariably includes that understanding in any deal, and wants to know where the money will come from, and when.

6. The money personality competes for real rewards either as a member of a group or as an individual.

7. The high social I.Q. necessary to the money personality is acquirable in four clearcut steps.

8. The money personality has a special, intense, meaningful interest in his work, and thereby creates wealth that never existed before.

9. The money personality is a giver of gifts as an automatic defense against the immature desire to be taken care of.

10. The money personality recognizes signals of success or failure and acts at once accordingly.

11. The money personality trains himself in a few key winning habits.

12. The money personality orients to money or to a winner.

A final few words for those who really want to head for the mountain tops.

Don't get a "thing" of your own.

Don't identify yourself to yourself as a doctor, a retailer, an author, an artist, accountant, producer, musician, manufacturer. Don't be any specific somebody.

Reject the idea that there is special "egoboo" in being a general manager or a creator of artistic things.

I've said this earlier. Now I make it the big thought. You can *do* any of those for a living, but don't *be* one. Transcend all jobs and professions—except one.

Make out your final white card to read:

I am a financier

Think and be(come) *that.*

How to Have Money and Be a Human Being

What I've said is only for success
In counting rooms and market places.
For your closest personal relations
You should find kinder solutions.

Remember: You can't take it with you.
P.S. The foregoing applies to people who are already super non-

victims. If you're a victim, it doesn't mean you until you have made your pile.

I realize that the twelve qualities I have described at length are probably useful to the person possessing them in other ways than for making and keeping money. But, as I see it, they are the practical aspects of human nature that create and maintain the wealth system of man.

The two negative things that emerge clearly from what I have observed is the moneymaking or moneykeeping weakness of the majority of males and the orientation weakness of women. The positive side of what I observed is of course more important.

The principal suggestion I have is that you use these ideas as constant reminders. Keep letting them tug you to proper action.

And so a cat looked at three kings. This that you have read is what he saw.

Bibliography of Success

Battle for the Mind, William Sargent. Doubleday, Garden City, N.Y., 1957. (The account by a psychiatrist of Pavlov's fatigue experiments.)

Be My Guest, Conrad Hilton. Prentice-Hall, Inc., Englewood Cliffs, N.J. 07632, 1957.

Bulls, Bears and Dr. Freud, Albert Haas and Don D. Jackson, M.D. World Publishing Co.

Business As a Game, Albert Z. Carr. New American Library.

Capital Appreciation in the Stock Market, Holmes. Parker Publishing Company, Inc., West Nyack, N.Y. 10994.

Classical Keynsian Price Theory and the Price Level, Sidney Weintraub. Chilton Company.

Double Your Money in Six Years, Burleigh. Parker Publishing Company, Inc., West Nyack, N.Y. 10994.

Drugs and the Mind, Robert S. DeRopp. St. Martin's Press, Inc.

The Evaluation of Common Stocks, Arnold Bernhard. Simon and Schuster.

Getting Rich with OPM, Sarnoff. Parker Publishing Company, Inc., West Nyack, N.Y. 10994.

The Golden Age, J. Paul Getty. Trident Press.

Grow Rich with Peace of Mind, Napoleon Hill. Hawthorne Books, Inc.

Happiness Is a Stock That Doubles in a Year, Ira V. Cobleigh. Bernard Geis Associates.

How I Turned One Thousand Dollars into a Million in Real Estate in My Spare Time, William Nickerson. Simon and Schuster.

How to Be Rich, J. Paul Getty. Trident Press.

How to Borrow Your Way to a Great Fortune, Hicks. Parker Publishing Company, Inc., West Nyack, N.Y. 10994.

How to Build a Second Income Fortune in Your Spare Time, Hicks. Parker Publishing Company, Inc., West Nyack, N.Y. 10994.

How to Earn a Fortune and Become Independent in Your Own Business, Dowd. Parker Publishing Company, Inc., West Nyack, N.Y. 10994.

How to Get More Business by Telephone, Jack Schwartz. Business Bourse.

How to Make Big Money at Home in Your Spare Time, Witt. Parker Publishing Company, Inc., West Nyack, N.Y. 10994.

How to Make Money Selling Stock Options, Asen and Asen. Parker Publishing Company, Inc., West Nyack, N.Y. 10994.

How to Make More Money, Marvin Small. Simon and Schuster.

How to Make $25,000 a Year Publishing Newsletters, Sheehan. Parker Publishing Company, Inc., West Nyack, N.Y. 10994.

How to Start Your Own Business on a Shoestring and Make Up to $100,000 a Year, Hicks. Parker Publishing Company, Inc., West Nyack, N.Y. 10994.

How to Win Friends and Influence People, Dale Carnegie.

Income Opportunities, Arco Publishing Company.

The Jewish Mystique, Ernest van den Haag. Stein and Day.

The Last Will and Testament, Robert Farmer. Arco Publishing Company.

The Magic of Believing, Claude M. Bristol. Prentice-Hall, Inc., Englewood Cliffs, N.J. 07632.

Master Plan for Financial Security, William Addison Watson. Watson Publishing Company.

Magic Mind Secrets for Building Great Riches Fast, Hicks. Parker Publishing Company, Inc., West Nyack, N.Y. 10994.

The Money Game, Adam Smith. Random House.

Mortgage Your Way to Wealth: The Principles of Supplemental

Financing, Steinberg. Parker Publishing Company, Inc., West Nyack, N.Y. 10994.

New York Times Guide to Personal Finance, San Nuccio.

101 Businesses You Can Start and Run with Less Than $1,000, Kahm. Parker Publishing Company, Inc., West Nyack, N.Y. 10994.

Poor Man, Rich Man, Herman Miller. Thomas Y. Crowell Company.

The Rich—Are They Different? George G. Kirstein, Houghton Mifflin Company, Boston.

The Richest Man in Babylon, George S. Clason. Hawthorn Books, Inc. (Contains "Seven Cures for a Lean Purse.")

The Secrets of Success Encyclopedia, Charles B. Roth. McGraw Hill.

Smart-Money Shortcuts to Becoming Rich, Hicks. Parker Publishing Company, Inc., West Nyack, N.Y. 10994.

Successful Moonlighting Techniques That Can Make You Rich, Frantz. Prentice-Hall, Inc., Englewood Cliffs, N.J. 07632.

Success Is As Easy As A—Ask; B—Believe; C—Cooperate; C—Compliment, M. R. Kopmeyer. Sherbourne Press, Inc., Los Angeles, Calif.

Think and Grow Rich, Napoleon Hill. Hawthorn Books, Inc.

21 Sure-Fire Ways to As Much As Double Your Income in One Year, Kinny and Kinney. Parker Publishing Company, Inc., West Nyack, N.Y. 10994.

Wealth Seeker's Guide, Southard. Parker Publishing Company, Inc., West Nyack, N.Y. 10994.

A Woman's Money: How to Protect and Increase It in the Stock Market, Brandt. Parker Publishing Company, Inc., West Nyack, N.Y. 10994.